WREATHS
for Every Season

by June Apel with Chalice Bruce

NORTH LIGHT BOOKS
CINCINNATI, OHIO
www.artistsnetwork.com

◆ ABOUT THE AUTHORS

June Apel crafts with her hands and her heart. She is known for her original, lovingly detailed creations—everything from wreaths and corn-husk dolls to quilts, sugar cookies and tole paint-ings. June lives in the quiet countryside of Indiana, Pennsylvania, with her husband Roger, Miss Martha the cat, two dogs and an assorted cast of barn cats. Stop by for a visit at www.juneapel.com.

June's daughter, **Chalice Bruce,** is a freelance writer and (as of this book) apprentice wreath-maker. She lives in Loveland, Ohio, with her husband Jeff, cat Baboo and wonder-dogs Dasher and Champ.

Other fine North Light Books are available from your local bookstore or art supply store or direct from the publisher.

06 05 04 03 02   5 4 3 2 1

Library of Congress Cataloging-in-Publication Data
Apel, June
  Wreaths for Every Season / by June Apel, with Chalice Bruce
    p. cm.
  Includes bibliographical references and index.
  ISBN 1-58180-239-0 (alk. paper)
  I. Wreaths. I. Bruce, Chalice. II. Title

TT899.75 .A63 2002
745.92'6–dc21

                    2001059076

EDITORS: Tricia Waddell and Jane Friedman
DESIGNER: Stephanie Strang
PRODUCTION COORDINATOR: Emily Gross and Sara Dumford
PRODUCTION ARTIST: Cheryl VanDeMotter
PHOTOGRAPHERS: Christine Polomsky, Tim Grondin and Al Parrish

metric conversion chart

TO CONVERT	TO	MULTIPLY BY
Inches	Centimeters	2.54
Centimeters	Inches	0.4
Feet	Centimeters	30.5
Centimeters	Feet	0.03
Yards	Meters	0.9
Meters	Yards	1.1
Sq. Inches	Sq. Centimeters	6.45
Sq. Centimeters	Sq. Inches	0.16
Sq. Feet	Sq. Meters	0.09
Sq. Meters	Sq. Feet	10.8
Sq. Yards	Sq. Meters	0.8
Sq. Meters	Sq. Yards	1.2
Pounds	Kilograms	0.45
Kilograms	Pounds	2.2
Ounces	Grams	28.4
Grams	Ounces	0.04

Create gorgeous gifts and decorations
WITH SILK AND DRIED FLOWERS!

◆ ◆ ◆ ◆ ◆ ◆ ◆ ◆ ◆ ◆ ◆ ◆ ◆ ◆ ◆ ◆

⟨ Whether you're planning a grand Thanksgiving dinner, a tropical theme party, or a romantic dinner for two, you'll find a wealth of creative silk and dried floral projects inside—each one designed to make your special occasions stand out. Terry Rye makes creating centerpieces easy, affordable and fun. The results are simply magnificent!

ISBN 1-55870-598-8, PAPERBACK, 128 PAGES, #70537-K

⟨ Capture the essence of the seasons with these simple, stunning floral arrangements. With a few basic techniques, a handful of materials, and a little creativity, you can make eye-pleasing accents for every room in your home. You'll find all the flower arranging advice you need inside, along with 15 projects using silk flowers, greenery, leaves, pinecones, gourds and more.

ISBN 1-58180-108-4, PAPERBACK, 96 PAGES, #31810-K

⟨ Whether you're the bride-to-be, a member of the wedding party, or a close friend, this book can show you how to create gorgeous floral arrangements for priceless wedding memories. You'll find guidelines for crafting 20 step-by-step projects, from the bride's bouquet and boutonnieres to pew decorations and wedding cake toppers.

ISBN 1-55870-560-0, PAPERBACK, 128 PAGES, #70488-K

Index

Dedications

I want to thank my Mom for teaching me the love of work, my husband for supporting that love, my children for their inspiration and my sister for always being there when I need her.

—June

To my co-author, Mum. I am so proud of you, your creative spirit, and your boundless, kind heart. Thank you for showing me how to make life a more beautiful place.

—Chalice

acknowledgments

♦　♦　♦　♦　♦　♦　♦　♦　♦　♦　♦　♦　♦　♦

HEARTFELT THANKS

to our favorite editor, Tricia Waddell, for her enthusiasm, encouragement and direction. To Christine Polomsky for making our photo shoot a little easier and a lot more fun than we expected. To Jamie for lending an artful hand, Laurie for always being there, and Champ, the world's best writing companion. To all my dear friends at Breeze for putting up with my late-night homework and for always being my best customers. And extra-special, hugs-and-kisses thanks to our ever-lovin', ever-patient husbands, Terry and Jeff, for holding our hands and believing in us. You make our wreaths go 'round!

Table of Contents

18
‹ The Spirit of Spring

50
Summer Glory ›

Wreaths Make the Seasons Go 'Round!

Living in the hills of Western Pennsylvania, surrounded by woods and cornfields, I am blessed with a perfect view of nature's annual journey from spring to winter and back again. It's a wondrous show to behold, and glorious inspiration for creating wreaths for every season. In this book, step by step and season by season, I'll show you how easy it is to make wreaths to brighten every room of your home, handmade gifts from your heart (the best kind!), and even your own original versions of wreaths you've admired in stores or catalogs, only for a lot less money. Along the way, I'll share favorite tricks I've learned in 30 years of wreathmaking—little ways to make your crafting more enjoyable and rewarding.

While materials lists and instructions detail precisely what you need to recreate each wreath as shown, use them as guidelines rather than rules. Take creative detours according to your own whims and fancies. I've included variations on every project to illustrate some of the endless possibilities. If, in the end, your wreath doesn't look exactly like mine, good for you! That means it's uniquely yours!

Making a wreath is a great way to pause and celebrate life's simple pleasures—nature's bounty, old-fashioned decorating romance, the satisfaction of creating something with your own hands. I hope the simple steps in this book will lead you far beyond the 20 projects featured here, into a joyful lifetime of wreathmaking.

Best wishes for season after season of celebration!

—June Apel

To help you choose the best wreath project based on the amount of time you want to devote and your skill level, use these helpful ratings at the beginning of each project. And don't be afraid to tackle the more challenging wreaths—the step-by-step photos and instructions will guide you through every project. Have fun!

TIME

🕑 Can be completed in an afternoon

🕑 🕑 Can be completed in a day

🕑 🕑 🕑 Can be completed in a weekend

DIFFICULTY

❀ **EASY** (You couldn't mess up if you tried!)

❀ ❀ **INTERMEDIATE** (A bit more involved, but you can do it!)

❀ ❀ ❀ **ADVANCED** (Requires a little extra patience and finesse.)

Wreathmaker's Toolkit

Wherever you find your inspiration—a stroll through the craft store, your own backyard or the pages of this book—this chapter will help you make the most of it. Here you'll find information on basic tools, techniques and supplies...everything you need to create your own one-of-a-kind wreaths!

Three Rules for Making Great Wreaths

◆ ◆ ◆ ◆ ◆ ◆ ◆ ◆ ◆ ◆ ◆ ◆ ◆ ◆ ◆

Okay, so they're more like suggestions than rules. Just keep them in mind and you can't go wrong.

1. DON'T SKIMP ◆ When I make a wreath, I like it to be substantial. Be generous with your flowers and other decorations. It's probably the easiest secret to good-looking wreaths.

2. BUILD TO LAST ◆ If you're going to make a wreath—especially if you're making it as a gift—take the time to do it right. Sometimes the smallest details like securing materials with glue *and* wire can make the difference between a wreath that lasts a few months and one that lasts a few years.

3. DON'T MIX MEDIA ◆ Mixing dried flowers and silk leaves on the same wreath creates an odd effect. Keep natural with natural and artificial with artificial.

Basic Supplies and Tools ›

Most craft stores carry the basic supplies and tools you need to create beautiful wreaths. You can also buy any hard-to-find materials from your local florist.

◆ **florist greening pins** Sometimes referred to as S-pins, greening pins are used for securing large flower heads, bows and other materials to your base. I always buy mine in bulk because I go through them so quickly.

◆ **florist wire (paddle wire)** Sold in a variety of gauges (the lower the gauge, the heavier the wire), florist wire comes in handy for a multitude of uses. A 28-gauge works well for most tasks, from making bundles to attaching materials to your base. The threadlike 30-gauge is nice for lightweight tasks where you want the wire to be inconspicuous, such as securing moss to a base or tying a bow. Use a heavier gauge wire for heavy-duty tasks, like attaching the branch in the Garden View Wreath (page 68) or making hanging loops. Keep a variety of colors (green, silver, black, gold) on hand and use whichever blends in best.

◆ **stem wire** This wire is used to add length to a flower stem and to make "picks." You can use heavier gauges for making hanging loops for your wreaths. The light, fabric-wrapped stem wire makes wonderful grapevine-like tendrils (see the Pumpkin Garland, page 88).

◆ **coiled florist wire** Because it doesn't kink like the paddle wire, I prefer using heavier-gauge coiled wire to make my hanging loops.

◆ **straight pins** Among other miscellaneous uses, pins are handy to use as an alternative to hot glue when working on foam forms. The shorter ones are most convenient.

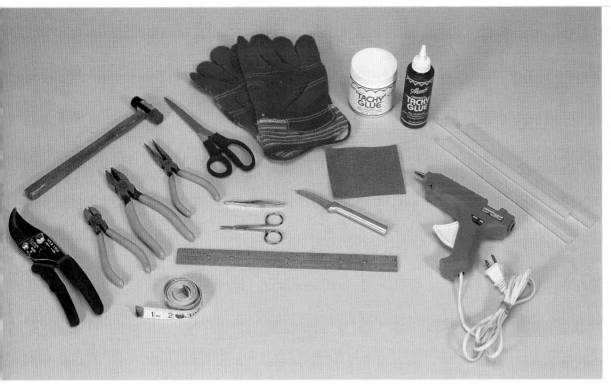

Tools (CLOCKWISE):

Gloves, craft glue, very fine sandpaper, small knife, glue gun and glue sticks, ruler, tweezers, cuticle scissors, tape measure, pruners, assorted pliers, tack hammer, scissors.

♦ **needle and thread** Always good to have on hand when you're working with fabrics and bows. You never know when you might need a stitch.

♦ **floral tape** This self-sealing tape is used for camouflaging wire stems and hanging loops.

♦ **twine, narrow ribbons and embroidery threads** Keep a variety of colors around for tying and attaching bows.

♦ **floral and acrylic spray paint** I occasionally use paint to perk up colors, to add bright silver and gold accents (buy the 14K kind for maximum sheen), and to salvage dried flowers or leaves that have lost their color but are in good condition otherwise. For best results, apply multiple light coats, allowing to dry after each coat.

‹TIP›

Spraying your materials in a cardboard box will help confine the overspray.

♦ **aroma oils** There are a multitude of scents from which to choose—floral, fruity, spicy, you name it. I prefer oils to aroma sprays because they're more economical. Aroma oils will stain flowers and ribbons, so be sure to apply carefully with an eyedropper to your base or other hidden area. Use sparingly—a drop or two is

all you need. (I've made wreaths that friends had to air out for a few days before hanging due to my overzealous aroma-ing!)

♦ **acrylic paint and paintbrush** Basic colors (white, green, brown) come in handy for disguising wires and raw edges. You'll need a variety of colors for the eggs in the Easter Basket Wreath (page 32), the birdhouse in the Garden View Wreath (page 68), and other hand-painted accents.

♦ **clear acrylic spray** Use sparingly. A couple of thin coats will help protect and preserve your dried flowers. It's an especially good idea for candle rings and other wreaths that will be handled and moved a lot. Expect a slight darkening of colors; test on individual flowers before spraying the whole wreath. You can use any finish, from matte to gloss, depending on the effect you're after.

♦ **glue gun and glue sticks** The glue gun is the MVP of wreathmaking tools! Don't bother buying the top-of-the-line—it will soon be covered with bits of dried flowers and moss. Do buy the longer glue sticks—they're a bit more economical, plus you don't have to stop as often to reload.

♦ **craft glue** Keep two types on hand: thicker glue in a jar for applying small, individual flow-

ers; and all-purpose glue in a bottle for other applications where fast drying is not a concern.

♦ **tweezers** Just the thing for working with delicate little flowers and for picking glue strings off your finished wreath.

♦ **scissors** At the very least, get a good pair of standard scissors for cutting ribbon. Small, cuticle-type scissors come in handy for detail work, like snipping small flowers, reshaping a leaf and trimming fine ribbons. I also keep utility shears for cutting fine wires.

♦ **assorted pliers** Needlenose pliers are especially useful for bending heavy wires and making hanging loops. You will also need a pair of wire-cutters for working with heavy wire and silk flower stems.

♦ **pruners** Handy for trimming thick dried flower stems and grapevines.

♦ **ruler or tape measure**

♦ **small knife** Handy for shaping florist foam.

♦ **gloves** A little extra protection for working with grapevines or thistles.

♦ **small tack hammer** For anchoring florist pins into fabric- or ribbon-covered foam bases.

♦ **very fine sandpaper** Among other random uses, I use sandpaper to touch up miniature birdhouses and other wooden accessories.

Choosing Your Base

♦♦♦ Choosing the right base for your wreath will not only make your wreath look its best, it will also make your crafting easier and more enjoyable. Here are some tips on working with the most common bases.

Straw >

This is my personal favorite. Not only are straw bases your cheapest option and easy to find in a wide range of sizes and shapes, they're also extremely versatile, easy to work with (they take gluing well and are easy to pin into), and appropriate for covering with anything from leaves to fabric. Straw bases are never perfectly round which, I think, only adds to the handcrafted charm of your finished wreath. Before you add a hanger or begin decorating, take a moment to decide on the most pleasing orientation of your wreath. Once you decide on the top, mark it with a piece of narrow ribbon that can be removed later.

Grapevine >

Grapevines are another inexpensive and fun base to work with. They offer a nice, wide surface area, plenty of places to wire your bundles, and lots of little nooks and crannies to tuck in decorations and stems. A grapevine wreath is a great choice if you're after a rustic or country look, or if you want to leave some of the base exposed, either left natural or spray painted for added color.

Grapevines come in many sizes and charming, irregular shapes. So, again, take a moment before you start decorating to decide which side you want to be the top. If you have access to grapevines, you can even make your base from scratch! (See page 34 for easy instructions.)

Foam >

If a nice, smooth finish and uniform shape is what you're after, a foam base is an excellent choice. This base works very well with lace and fabrics, lending itself to polished, Victorian looks. It also works well with silk flowers to make a lightweight wreath—especially nice for people with plastered walls who prefer using adhesive hooks to nails.

Because the foam is so dense, you may need to use your trusty tack hammer to insert florist pins, especially when your wreath is covered with fabric or ribbon. Hot glue will melt the foam, so opt for a low-temperature glue gun.

Metal Ring >

Sold at most craft stores, these welded rings are perfect when you need a strong, thin, perfectly round base—especially for horizontal formats like the Lilac Picnic Chandelier (page 52) and the Pumpkin Garland (page 88). They're also fun to use in combination with another wreath base. (See Sugarplums Wreath, page 124.)

Bay Leaf and Other Ready-to-Decorate Bases >

If a quick and easy wreath is what you want, consider starting with a plain base of bay leaves, lemon leaves, pine, cedar, pussy willow, grasses, baby's breath… the list goes on and on. It's the most expensive of the base options discussed here. To make sure you're getting the most for your money, give the wreath a gentle shake to check for excessive shedding and to make sure leaves are attached securely.

Etc. >

Keep your eyes open for unusual and unconventional wreath opportunities, like the Terra Cotta Pot Topper (page 74) or ways to make your own base, like the Americana Wreath (page 64). Wooden curtain hoops make great little bases for miniature wreaths; use them to cheer up cabinets, table settings and gift wraps.

Hanging Tips

♦ ♦ ♦ ♦ ♦ ♦ ♦ ♦ ♦ ♦ ♦ ♦ ♦ ♦ ♦ ♦ ♦ ♦ ♦ ♦

♦ Be sure to position your hanging wires far down enough so they won't be visible from the front of your finished wreath.

♦ One hanger or two? Use two if your wreath is especially heavy, or if it's a heart or some other odd shape that's hard to balance with one hanging wire.

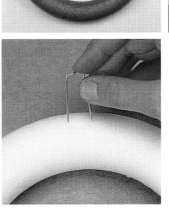

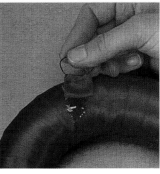

Adding hanging tabs.
Use this type of hanger for any ribbon- or fabric-covered base. Make a ring out of florist wire. (Wrap the wire around two fingers three times; on the fourth pass, twist the wire around the ring to secure.) Cut a short length* of ribbon. Fold in the raw ends to meet in the center and glue them down. Slip the ring onto your ribbon, and glue the ribbon in half. Glue the tab to the back of your wreath.

* The size of your finished tab should be proportionate to the size of your wreath—big enough to secure to and support your wreath, yet small enough so that the hoop doesn't show from the front of your wreath.

Straw: Adding a Hanger
Store-bought wreath hangers work well with straw bases. Put a dab of hot glue on the points of the hanger, insert, and glue again to secure. Alternately, it's also easy to make your own hanger. Simply slide your wire through the straw several times, forming a loop, then secure with glue.

Grapevine: Adding a hanger
Cut a generous length of wire, around 10" (25cm), and secure one end by twisting it around a few vines. Bend your wire to create the hanging hoop, and secure the other end in the same manner. Trim off excess wire. Use floral tape to cover any sharp points and camouflage the hanger.

Foam: Adding a hanger
Dip a floral pin in thick craft glue and insert into your wreath at a 45° angle, using a tack hammer as necessary. Squeeze on a dab of hot glue to secure. This type of hanger is only appropriate for a relatively lightweight wreath.

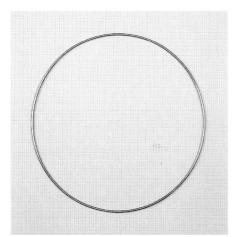

Metal Ring

Bay Leaf Wreath

Pine Wreath

Selecting Flowers

The Dried Wreath ›

Dried plants—flowers, grasses, pods, foliage, etc.—are my favorite wreathmaking materials. I love the natural look and smell of them. I love gathering and drying my own. And I love the variety of colors and textures—from the earthy tones of goldenrod, ferns and mosses to the cheerful shades of larkspur and peonies, from delicate delphiniums to sassy sunflowers. I even enjoy the way the colors of a dried flower wreath fade and mellow over time, creating a cozy "antique" patina. It's like having a whole new wreath!

You can reasonably expect a dried flower wreath to hold its color and shape for up to a year. To avoid premature fading, display your wreath away from direct sunlight. Flip to page 17 for simple ways to revive your wreath when it does start showing its age.

The Silk Wreath ›

Today's craft stores offer a staggering variety of silk flowers, foliage and artifical berries—a virtual garden of wreathmaking materials from which to pick! Silk wreaths outlive dried wreaths, holding their colors and shapes for several years—although they, too, will fade if displayed in direct sunlight. Silk wreaths are an appropriate choice for bathrooms, front doors and other sheltered outdoor displays.

Quality silk flowers don't come cheap, however, you can save money just by thinking ahead. Craft stores typically operate a season ahead of the rest of the world, so picks and flowers commonly go on sale early in the season. And you'll find even better deals at the end of the season and after holidays. With a quick spray of silver, those clearance-priced spring berries would be dandy in your Let-It-Snow Chandelier (page 130).

Caring for Your Wreath ›

An occasional dusting will help keep your wreath looking its best. A small paintbrush is the safest option for dried flower wreaths. For silk wreaths you could try using a hairdryer (on the lowest setting), short bursts of pressurized air (the kind you use to clean computer keyboards) or a silk flower cleaner. If your bow looks flat, plump it up with a warm curling iron.

Dried, Preserved or Freeze-Dried?

◆ ◆

SILICA GEL PRESERVED
Silica gel preserves the natural colors and shapes of flowers for a close-to-fresh look.

AIR-DRIED
Air-drying plants darkens the colors, changes the shapes, and results in a beautiful look very distinct from the fresh version. This is the most durable and longest lasting of these three options, and easy to do yourself.

FREEZE-DRIED
The most expensive of these three procedures, freeze-drying comes closest to maintaining that "fresh flower" color and shape.

Favorite Flowers for Air-Drying

◆ ◆ ◆ ◆ ◆ ◆ ◆ ◆ ◆ ◆ ◆ ◆ ◆ ◆ ◆ ◆ ◆

amaranth ◆ artemesia ◆ baby's breath ◆ caspia ◆ celosia ◆ coneflower (I dry primarily for the centers—the petals will not keep their shape) ◆ dill ◆ dusty miller ◆ everlastings ◆ feverfew ◆ fountain grasses ◆ goldenrod ◆ holly ◆ hydrangea ◆ ivy ◆ larkspur ◆ lavender ◆ nigella ◆ peonies (even though it breaks my heart to cut them off the bush!) ◆ pussy willow ◆ Queen Anne's lace ◆ roses ◆ common sage ◆ statice ◆ strawflower (it's especially important to pick and hang these just as they're beginning to open) ◆ sweet Annie ◆ tansy ◆ wheat ◆ yarrow

Basic Techniques

Bundling ▷

Bundling will give your wreath a full, well-balanced look. It's also a far more efficient alternative to attaching flowers one by one. Sometimes you'll make bundles of the same type flower, as in the Sherbet Pinwheel Wreath (page 38). More often, you'll make mixed bundles. Note: Some flowers, such as sanfordii, are too fragile to bundle; it's best to add these flowers individually toward the end.

Continuous Wiring ▷

This is a quick and handy technique for covering your base with flower bundles, as well as artificial picks, moss and other materials. Start by securing the end of your paddle wire around your base. Glue a row of flower bundles to your wreath, and wrap the wire taut across the stems and around the back of your wreath. Place the next row of bundles so that their heads hide the stems of the previous bundles. Wrap with wire. Continue until your wreath is completely covered. Cut and fasten the wire, and secure with a dab of hot glue.

Working With Hydrangea ▷

I use a lot of hydrangea in my wreaths, both as a filler and as a feature flower. It's nice and full, comes in a variety of colors, and is relatively inexpensive. It's also very fragile, so here are a few tips to make working with hydrangea a little easier.

Bundling and wiring
When making bundles using an assortment of flowers or grasses, keep the longer, spikier ones in back; the rounder, fuller ones in middle; and the smallest ones in front. The size of your bundles should be in proportion to the size of your wreath. Secure the stems with a few twists of 28-gauge florist wire.

Attaching hydrangea to your wreath
Break large hydrangea heads into smaller pieces—they're easier to work with this way, plus you can cover more area. Apply hot glue to your wreath, set the hydrangea in place, and secure it at the stem with a florist pin. Hold in place and apply light pressure for thirty seconds or so, just until the glue sets.

Touching up bare spots
Hydrangea will shed as you work with it. Don't just throw away these individual florets, use them to fill in bare spots. Apply using tacky glue and tweezers.

Bowmaking 101

Too many people are intimidated by the prospect of making a bow. Fact is, if you can make a loop and tie a knot, you've got what it takes to make a fabulous bow! If there is a "secret" to bowmaking, it's this: Use wired ribbon. Really. You simply can't make a bad bow with wired ribbon. You'll probably pay more than you would for non-wired ribbon, but it's so easy to shape and such a joy to work with that the extra investment is well worth it.

The Stacked Bow >

Nine times out of ten, I use some variation of this basic "stacked" bow. All you do is make two easy-as-pie bows and tie them together to form one nice, full bow.

But wait—it gets even better! Once you get the hang of it, you can make little adjustments and variations to create all kinds of bows! Create a layered look by using a satin bow on the bottom and a sheer ribbon on top. Work with four or five narrow ribbons at once to create a confetti-type bow like the one I use on the Sherbet Pinwheel Wreath (page 38). To create a bigger, fuller bow, simply make more loops per layer. Bigger yet? Just add more layers. The bow possibilities are endless…and, in these five simple steps, yours for the making!

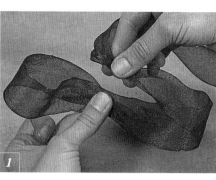

step 1
Begin by making two loops to establish the width of your bow.

step 2
Make two more loops of roughly the same size.

step 3
With a generous length of narrow ribbon, tie off the center of your bow tightly. (Don't trim off this ribbon yet, you'll be using it in step 5.) Cut the tail of your bow to the desired length. You now have the bottom layer of your bow.

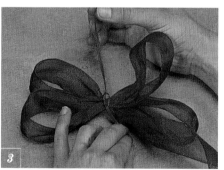

step 4
Repeat steps 1 and 2, making a second four-looped bow slightly smaller than the first one. This will form the top layer of your bow.

step 5
Tie the two layers together using the tails of the narrow ribbon from step 3, keeping the knot on the back of your bow. Trim off the narrow ribbon or use it to attach your bow to your wreath. Arrange and fluff the loops, and there you have it…a beautiful, professional-looking bow! I knew you could do it!

The Flat Bow >

Here's another easy bow to make when you want a simple, understated effect.

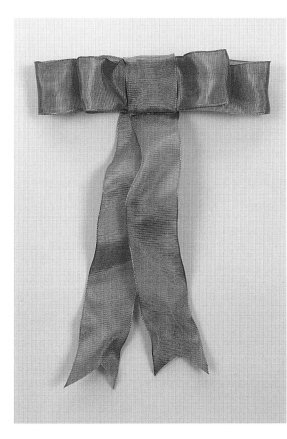

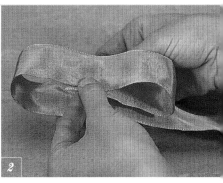

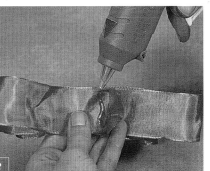

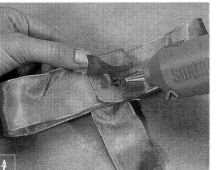

step 1
Bring in one end of your ribbon to make a loop. Secure the end with a dab of glue.

step 2
Make a second, equal loop and secure in the center with glue. If you like, you can use a pin to mark the center of your bow.

step 3
Make a second set of loops slightly larger than the first. Again, secure in the middle with glue.

step 4
Cut a length of ribbon approximately three times the ribbon's width. Glue one end to the back of your bow.

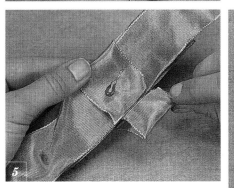

step 5
Bring the ribbon around the front of your bow, fold under the raw edge and glue down on the back of your bow.

step 6
Cut another length of ribbon twice as long as you want the tails. Fold this ribbon in half at a slight angle and glue to the back of your bow.

step 7
Finish off tails by folding the ribbon in half and cutting at an angle.

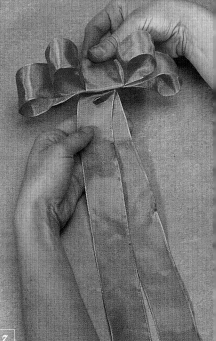

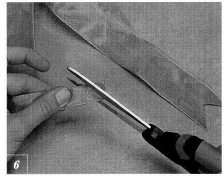

The Overlay Bow >

Say you find the perfect sheer ribbon for your wreath, only its pattern gets lost in a regular stacked bow. I have just the trick for you! You'll need equal lengths of a sheer ribbon and a base ribbon which should be in a coordinating color that accentuates the sheer ribbon's pattern.

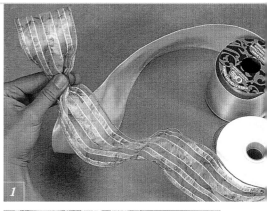

step 1

Layer your sheer ribbon on top of your base ribbon. Follow the directions on page 14 for making a stacked bow.

step 2

Finish your bow by squeezing a few drops of glue along the edges of the tails to secure the two ribbons together.

step 3

Make a loop of ribbon and secure the ends with glue.

step 4

Tie the glued seam of your loop with a length of narrow ribbon and attach to the center of your bow.

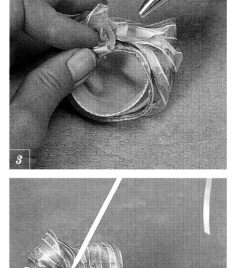

Wreath Makeovers

No matter how carefully you construct your wreath and how diligent you are to keep it out of direct sunlight, the day will come when your wreath starts showing its age. Just a few minutes of attention might make a world of difference. Here are a few tricks to revive a tired wreath:

♦ Replace the bow. Sometimes a fresh ribbon is all that's needed.

♦ Give it a little "trim." Simply snip off any stems that are broken or flowers that are faded. (Great additions to potpourri!)

♦ Replace key flowers that are faded or discolored, or simply add new flowers.

♦ A can of spray paint can go a long way, as the following makeovers illustrate.

♦ If your wreath is just too far gone, be sure to salvage any pods, berries, picks, etc. you might use in a future wreath.

Summer-to-Winter Makeover >

Before
This lemon-leaf base was a fine little decoration for my kitchen—until, that is, the leaves turned a drab brown and the roses faded.

After
First, I sprayed the entire wreath gold, roses and all. I added some silver accents (baker's fern and pinecones), a few pink pepperberries and finished with glitter and a bow.

Winter-to-Spring Makeover >

Before
This spruce wreath was my best buy of the season! It held all its needles through winter and beyond. Come spring, it was still in perfect condition, but almost completely drained of color. Besides, who ever heard of a spring evergreen wreath?

After
I sprayed the wreath a pretty yellow…added a ring of spring blooms—roses, veronica, rice flower, larkspur and hops—and voila! I'm the only house in the neighborhood with a spring spruce wreath!

The Spirit of Spring

◆◆◆ Winter softens into spring. I love the simple things about this time of the year—wild violets freckling woodland floors, the return of familiar birdsongs, the smell of green in the air. Time to open the windows wide and let the fresh air in!

Nothing airs out and perks up a room like your very own handmade wreath. Go with soft pastels and cheery colors for springtime. Incorporate the season's most jubilant blooms—tulips, daffodils, peonies, hydrangea, cherry blossoms and pansies. Add spring floral scents of violet, lilac, hyacinth and lily of the valley (Just a hint, like it's drifting in on a breeze).

The wreaths in this chapter are guaranteed to breathe the spirit of spring into your home. I recommend the Sherbet Pinwheel for playful souls, the Picture of Spring for artistic types, and the Spring Medley for those whose thoughts turn to romance this time of year. You'll also find a sweet-as-sugar Easter wreath, and the pretty and practical Keepsake Wreath—just the project for a rainy April day.

(above) EASTER BASKET WREATH; (opposite page starting from upper left, clockwise) SPRING MEDLEY, KEEPSAKE WREATH, SHERBERT PINWHEEL WREATH, PICTURE OF SPRING

Spring Medley

♦♦♦ ANY ROOM WILL FEEL A LITTLE SUNNIER WITH THIS SUMPTUOUS MEDLEY OF BLOOMS— THE FANCY, CASCADING BOW IS SIMPLY ICING ON THE CAKE! THIS STYLE OF LEMON LEAF WREATH IS VERY POPULAR THESE DAYS; YOU'LL SEE THEM IN VIRTUALLY EVERY HOME DECO- RATING CATALOG FOR ANYWHERE FROM $50 TO $120, DEPENDING ON THE SIZE AND COMPLEXITY (THIS SPRING MEDLEY WOULD PROBABLY RUN AROUND $90). ·BETWEEN YOU AND ME, IT'S RELATIVELY EASY TO MAKE (YES, EVEN THE BOW!)—AND FOR A LOT LESS MONEY. JUST THINK: YOU DON'T HAVE TO PAY FOR SHIPPING, PLUS YOU GET THE PLEASURE OF MAKING IT YOURSELF!

TIME

DIFFICULTY

2 straw wreaths: one 14" (36cm) and one 18" (46cm)—try to find wreaths that fit together snugly (see step 1)

9-12 dried peonies (pink)

3 heads dried hydrangea (light green)

6-9 dried rose heads (yellow)

nigella orientalis

starflowers (natural)

larkspur (white)

rice flower (white)

sanfordii

silver queen sage

ti tree (pink)

lemon leaves (salal)

feather fern

pepperberries (pink)

5 yards (4.5m) of 1½" (4cm) wired taffeta ribbon (pink) for bow

florist wire

florist pins

hot glue gun

Substitute Your Favorites

♦ ♦ ♦ ♦ ♦ ♦ ♦ ♦ ♦ ♦ ♦ ♦ ♦ ♦ ♦ ♦ ♦

• **FEATURE FLOWERS**: freeze-dried roses, magnolias, crabapples
• **"RADIATING" FLOWERS**: amaranthus, baby eucalyptus, fescue grass, flax, heather, lavender, lepto, pennyroyal, bracken fern, flowering oregano
• **FILLER FLOWERS**: Australian daisies, feverfew, lemon mint, rodanthe, coxcomb, yarrow, hops, globe amaranth, strawberry flowers

step 1

Make the double base. Press the smaller wreath flush inside the larger wreath. Glue along the seam, and wire to secure. Attach a wire for hanging (see page 11).

Secret to Success

◆ ◆ ◆ ◆ ◆ ◆ ◆ ◆ ◆ ◆ ◆ ◆ ◆ ◆ ◆ ◆

As you add each type of flower, arrange them first and glue in place only when you're happy with the placement and spacing. Use florist pins as needed.

Puff Up Your Peonies

◆ ◆ ◆ ◆ ◆ ◆ ◆ ◆ ◆ ◆ ◆ ◆ ◆ ◆ ◆ ◆

If your dried peonies are a little too "mushed," steam them just until the petals start to soften, then blow into the center to puff open. Stand upright and allow to dry.

step 2

Build a base of lemon leaves. Using a dab of hot glue (and florist pins as needed), secure the base of each leaf to the straw base. Fill in the outer and inner edges first, then fill in between, placing leaves in random directions. Completely cover the straw base.

step 3

Add peonies and hydrangea. Cut the peony stems to about 3" (8cm). Evenly space three clusters of peonies around your wreath. Glue and insert stems into the straw. (If you're having trouble, use a screwdriver to poke the holes.) For added dimension, let your peonies sit above the lemon leaves rather than nestling them. Center a head of hydrangea between each cluster of peonies; break one of the heads in half, leaving room in between to add your bow later. (See page 13 for special tips on working with hydrangea.)

step 4

Add roses. Evenly place roses in clusters of three or four. (Don't forget to save that space for your bow!) Glue into place.

step 5

Add nigella and starflowers. Break off sprigs of nigella and cluster in a few spots around the inner perimeter of your wreath. Make bundles of starflowers and insert them randomly around the center and inside edge

step 6

Add larkspur. Cut the larkspur into 3" to 4" (8cm to 10cm) sprigs and cluster around the outside of your wreath, establishing a radiating effect that will be accentuated with the flowers to follow.

step 7

Add rice flowers and sanfordii. Make small bundles of rice flowers. Use these bundles and sprigs of sanfordii to fill in around the peonies, roses and hydrangea. (You're still saving room for your bow, right?)

step 8
Add silver queen sage and ti tree. Make 3" to 5" (8cm to 13cm) bundles of silver queen sage and ti tree, and arrange in a radiating pattern around the outside of your wreath.

step 9
Add feather fern. Break off 3" to 5" (8cm to 13cm) pieces of feather fern and work them in along the outer perimeter of your wreath. (It's always best to add your most delicate drieds toward the end.)

step 10
Add pepperberries. Almost done! For the final dried element, add small clusters of pepperberries randomly around your wreath, filling in any holes.

step 11
Now for the bow. There's a simple secret to this lush, sprawling bow: Make two stacked bows with 15" to 20" (38cm to 51cm) tails and "stagger" them in the space you've been saving. Use glue and a florist pin per bow to secure.

step 12
Arrange the tails. Finesse the tails to cascade down and around your wreath, tucking under flowers here and there. Use florist pins in strategic places to secure—just be sure they are hidden by your flowers.

♦♦♦ The Spring Medley…
instant sunshine!

Lemon leaves quickly lose their color in direct sunlight, so choose a nice, sheltered spot to display your beautiful Spring Medley. If you really enjoy this style of wreath, don't stop at spring. You can follow the same basic steps to create a medley for any season! The only rule is to have one featured element—in this case, the peonies. Try sunflowers for summer, yarrow for fall, and pomegranates for winter! For the other flowers, just aim for a variety of textures and sizes.

variation

Go monotone!

This is a wonderful wreath to do in a monotone scheme. For my "shades of white" variation, I featured freeze-dried gardenias, artemesia, eucalyptus leaves and starched antique lace.

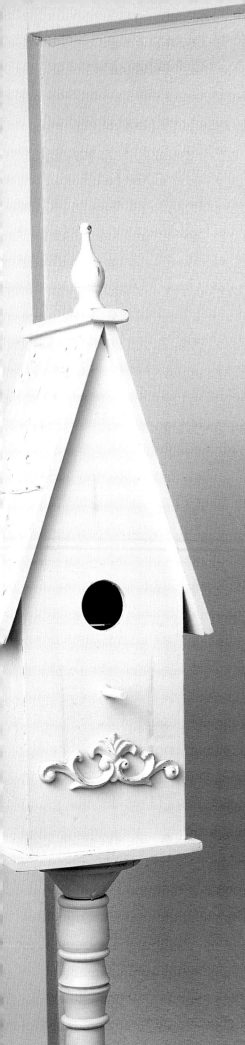

Picture of Spring

what you'll need

♦♦♦ SPRING IS FOREVER BLOOMING IN THIS GLEEFUL LITTLE TRIO! IT'S THREE TIMES THE FUN—A WONDERFUL WAY TO START YOUR WREATHMAKING YEAR, A GREAT DECORATIVE SOLUTION FOR ANY NARROW, HARD-TO-DECORATE WALL AND A SUPER SPRINGTIME GIFT. DESPITE THE INTRICATE APPEARANCE, IT IS RELATIVELY EASY AND INEXPENSIVE TO MAKE, ESPE-CIALLY IF YOU USE LEFTOVER ROSES FROM YOUR CHRISTMAS CRAFTING. THE HARDEST PART IS DECIDING HOW TO DISPLAY YOUR TRIO. WILL IT BE THE RIB-BON? THE FRAME? BOTH? I COULDN'T MAKE UP MY MIND, SO I'LL LET YOU DECIDE FOR YOURSELF!

TIME

🕐 🕐 🕐

DIFFICULTY

✖

three 6" (15cm) foam wreaths

assorted dried flowers in various stages of bloom: spray roses (pinks and white), larkspur or delphinium (white, blue, pink), Australian daisies, ammobium (yellow), plus a few miniature rosebuds

1 large bunch of preserved evergreen ming fern

10 yards of inexpensive, 1" (2.5cm) ribbon (green)

3 yards of 1½" (4cm) wired ribbon for bow (optional)

3 small buttons (optional)

picture frame, opening should measure no less than 8" x 24" (20cm x 61cm)

6 brads

fishing line

sharp knife

florist wire

tweezers

craft glue

acrylic spray

hot glue gun

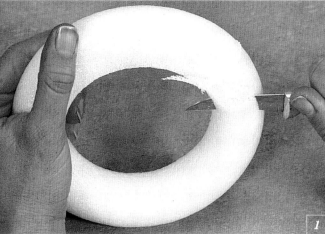

step 1

Flatten the backs. Use a knife to carefully slice about one-third off the back of each wreath. This will make them sit nicely against the wall.

‹NOTE›

Some craft stores sell foam wreaths that come with one flat side. This will save you a step.

step 2

Wrap in ribbon. Wrap each wreath with green ribbon, securing the beginnings and ends of your ribbon with a dab of hot glue. Add a tab at the top of each wreath for hanging (see page 11).

step 3

Make ming bundles. Cut your ming into short sprigs. Use florist wire to tie small bundles about the size of large grapes.

step 4

Cover wreaths with ming. Work your way around the front of each wreath, hiding the stem of each ming bundle behind the head of the next. Cover wreaths #1 and #2 solidly, creating a lush, grassy-looking surface. For wreath #3, just be sure to cover the inner and outer perimeters well; you can be sparing in between. Use scissors to neaten your ming as necessary.

step 5

Separate flowers by bloom-stage. Separate each type of flower into three groupings: buds (for wreath #1), partially opened flowers (for wreath #2) and full blooms (for wreath #3). Take care not to mix up your flowers; decorate each wreath only with its designated bloom-stage.

Timesaver

◆ ◆

For a different look that's much quicker
to achieve, cover your trio with soft sheet moss
or reindeer moss instead of ming.

◆ WREATH #1

step 7

First, wreath #1. Using tweezers and craft glue, add sprigs of larkspur around the rose clusters.

step 8

Add ammobium buds, mini rosebuds and some Australian daisy buds, and wreath #1 is done! Apply a light coat of acrylic spray.

tip

If your larkspur is too delicate to dip in glue, carefully squeeze a drop of glue directly on the wreath and use tweezers to set the flowers in place.

step 6

Start with the roses. Arrange and glue your roses in six groupings around your first two wreaths. Be extra generous with the roses on wreath #3. Next, take each individual wreath to completion.

◆ WREATH #2

step 9

Now onto wreath #2. Fill in around the roses with larkspur.

step 10

In go the ammobium.

step 11

And finally the Australian daisies. Finish with a light coat of acrylic spray. Two wreaths down, one to go!

step 12

Now for wreath #3. This time, cover virtually the entire wreath with larkspur, allowing the ming to peek out around the inner and outer edges.

step 13

Add ammobium, fill in any holes with Australian daisies, and wreath #3 should be drenched in blooms! Don't forget the acrylic spray.

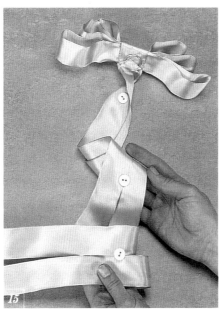

step 14

Frame the wreaths. Arrange the trio within your inverted frame. When you're happy with the spacing, use a ruler to mark off the top of each wreath on both sides of the frame. These marks indicate where to nail brads; be sure to leave enough sticking out so you can string fishing line horizontally from brad to brad, making it as taut as possible. Suspend the wreaths by bending the hanging loops downward to hook over the fishing line.

step 15

Add ribbon hanger. Instead of (or in addition to) framing your trio, you could display them on a pretty ribbon. Make a flat bow (see page 15) with long, 30" (76cm) tails. Arrange your trio vertically along the tails and mark off the top of each wreath. Stitch a button at each point, being certain to catch the inner edge of each tail in your stitches. Hang the wreaths on the buttons.

♦♦♦ Three cheers for your Picture of Spring!
Aren't your little wreaths beautiful? This simple format—themed groupings of small wreaths—offers endless variations, both in the materials you use and how you choose to display your finished wreaths. You could make a multi-colored trio of rosebud hearts and display them horizontally on a small branch. Create a variety of kitchen-herb samplers to adorn your cabinet doors. Or make a four-seasons quartet using artificial floral mini-picks—daffodils for spring, sunflowers for summer, leaves for fall, and poinsettias for winter.

variation

A merry little foursome!
Cover each small foam heart with a different type of preserved greenery, such as cedar, baker's fern, juniper and boxwood. Create the snow-dusted look by lightly drybrushing with white acrylic paint or liquid snow. I decorated my foursome with mini pinecones, jingle bells, brunia and coordinating bows.

Easter Basket Wreath

◆◆◆ HERE'S A NEAT TWIST ON WREATHMAKING. FIRST, I'LL SHOW YOU HOW TO MAKE YOUR OWN GRAPEVINE WREATH FROM SCRATCH. THEN YOU'LL SEE HOW TO TURN YOUR ORDINARY WREATH INTO A FUN-FILLED EASTER BASKET—A CHARMING DECORATION FOR FRONT DOOR, CHILD'S ROOM OR BUNNY TRAIL! FOR ADDED FUN, GET YOUR FAVORITE KIDS TO PITCH IN AND PAINT THE EGGS. SAVE A FEW FROM EACH YEAR (BE SURE TO MARK NAMES AND YEARS DISCRETELY ON THE BOTTOMS) AND BESTOW THEM ON THE KIDS WHEN THEY'RE OLDER AS THE START OF THEIR OWN FAMILY EASTER TRADITION.

TIME

DIFFICULTY

17" (43cm) metal ring

ten to fifteen 5' (1.5m) grapevines

8 stems silk tulips
(assorted spring colors)

artificial grass

stuffed Easter bunny and baby peep

miniature basket

12 decorated eggs (wood, ceramic or
papier maché, the lighter the better)

3 yards (2.7m) of 2½" (6.3cm)
ribbon for bow

24" (61cm) of 2½" (6cm) lace
with one decorative edge

7 yards (6.3m) of 1½" (3.8cm) plisse
ribbon (yellow); you can substitute
grosgrain or any ribbon with body

20" x 20" (51cm x 51cm) piece of
chicken wire; your hardware store
will cut it for you by the yard, or
buy it pre-packaged at a craft store

2 pieces of cardboard, about 20" x 12"
(51cm x 30cm) each

2 blocks of florist foam

white masking tape

brown florist tape

florist wire

duct tape

hot glue gun

Save a Step

◆ ◆ ◆ ◆ ◆ ◆ ◆ ◆ ◆ ◆ ◆ ◆ ◆ ◆ ◆ ◆

I'll show you how to create your own base out of grapevines, but you can get the same general effect by purchasing an oval grapevine wreath, about 20" x 15" (51cm x 38cm). Get the narrowest diameter you can find so your basket "handle" doesn't look out of proportion.

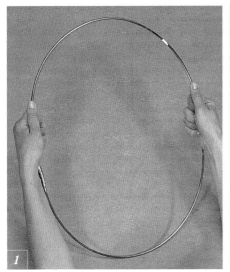

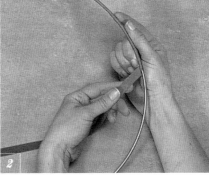

step 1
Shape hoop. Wrap duct tape around the weld of your metal ring to keep it from splitting. With the taped joint on the side, squeeze the ring into an oval shape.

step 2
Wrap hoop with tape. Wrap the entire hoop in brown florist tape so you won't notice it through the grapevines.

step 3
Entwine hoop with grapevine. Start by wiring on the end of a grapevine and wrapping it firmly around your hoop. (Use heavier vines first, saving the finer vines for the top layers of your wreath.) Take your time, pruning off any wild, unwieldy offshoots as you go. But try to save as many curlicues as possible—they'll add a nice sense of whimsy to your basket.

Before You Start
♦ ♦ ♦ ♦ ♦ ♦ ♦ ♦ ♦ ♦ ♦ ♦ ♦ ♦

Soak grapevines in water for one hour or, better yet, overnight. This makes them much more flexible and easier to work with.

step 4
Wrap, wrap, wrap. To start a new grapevine, tuck the end under previous vines and continue wrapping, always in the same direction. Continue until your grapevine wreath is about 1½" to 2" (3.8cm to 5cm) in diameter. Select the best-looking side to be the "handle" (or top) of your basket. Turn over and attach wire for hanging (see page 11).

step 5
Cut your basket. Wearing heavy gloves for protection, fold your chicken wire in half; you should now have a 10" x 20" (25cm x 50cm) piece. Carefully cut out the shape of your basket, using the bottom half of your wreath as a guide and adding about an inch (2.5cm) all around.

step 6
"Sew" chicken wire in place. Shape your chicken wire basket, bending it around to "hug" the grapevine. Flip your wreath over and use florist wire to tack the chicken wire to the grapevine every 3" to 4" (8cm to 10cm), starting at the top corner and working all the way around.

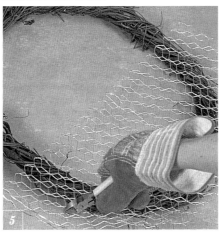

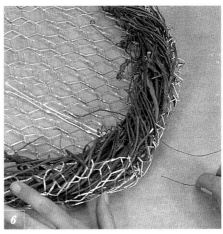

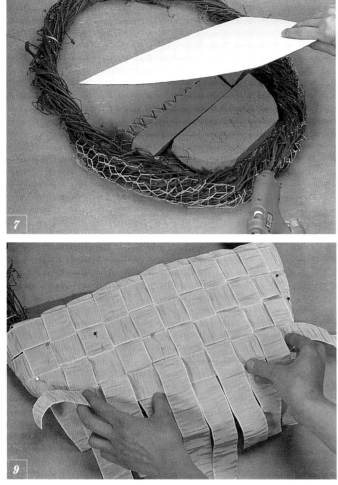

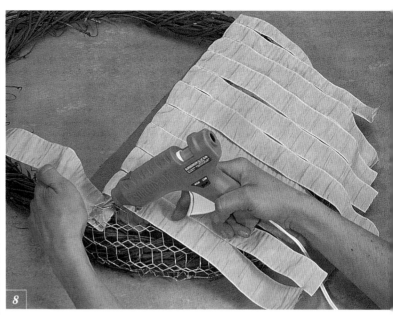

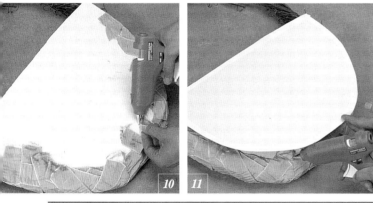

step 7

Finish basket base. Again using the bottom half of your wreath as a guide, cut both pieces of cardboard to size, this time adding about an inch (2.5cm) above the top of the chicken wire. Cut blocks of florist foam to fill the inside of your basket. Glue one of your cardboard pieces to the back of your wreath. Allow to dry, using weight or clamps to ensure a good, tight bond.

step 8

Attach vertical ribbons. For the vertical weaves of your basket, cut eight lengths of plisse ribbon at 14" (36cm) and four lengths at 10" (25cm). With the longer pieces in the center, arrange your ribbons across your chicken wire frame; the ribbons should butt against each other, and there should be at least ½" (1.3cm) overhang at the top and bottom of your basket. Secure only the top of each ribbon with a fine line of glue right where the ribbon folds behind the chicken wire. If you glue too far down there won't be room for your first horizontal weave.

step 9

Weave your basket. For the horizontal weaves, cut three lengths of plisse ribbon at 23" (58cm) and three lengths at 18" (46cm). Using the longer pieces at the top of your basket, weave into your vertical ribbons; there should be at least a ½" (1.3cm) overhang on either side. Cut additional lengths of ribbon as needed to completely cover the height of your basket.

step 10

Secure loose ends. Make sure all your ribbons form a nice, tight weave. Then turn your wreath over and glue down the loose ends to the cardboard. (If you want to be very diligent and ensure an extra-long life for your basket, use a needle and thread to tack each corner of your weave.)

step 11

Finish the back. Use masking tape to finish off the edge of your second piece of cardboard and glue in place on the back of your wreath. Again, clamp or weigh down and allow to dry.

step 12

"Plant" tulips. Now the real fun begins! Arrange tulips on one side of your wreath, inserting the stems into the florist foam.

step 13

Position and secure bunny. Snuggle your bunny into your tulips and carefully glue him into place.

step 14

Add mini-basket and build egg base. Glue your bunny's basket into place. Cut a few small pieces of florist foam and glue into the right side of your basket to serve as a base for your eggs.

step 15

Trim with lace. Carefully glue the lace along the top edge of your basket, securing both ends around the back of the wreath.

step 16

Pile in your eggs. Position your eggs and hot glue them into place. It's easiest to arrange half of them as the base layer, then stack your favorites on top.

step 17

Fill in with grass. Fill in around your bunny and eggs with little tufts of artificial grass. (The handle of a paintbrush comes in handy for tucking grass into tight spots!) Trim any unruly excess.

step 18

Add the bow. Make a bow. (I used an overlay bow—see page 16 for instructions.) Use a stem of wire, slipped through the back of your bow and bent in half, to secure your bow in the florist foam at the base of your tulips. Place your little peep into bunny's basket and you're done!

♦♦♦ Have a happy holiday with your Easter Basket!
If the bunny is a little too cute for your taste, leave him out and add more flowers. If you're making this as a gift, just pin Mr. Bunny in place so he can be removed later, and tuck some real candies into the mini-basket!

variation

Harvest Basket
For a rustic fall variation of the basket wreath, replace the ribbon with woven cornhusk—either natural or fabric-dyed, as I've used here. Fill with crabapples, gourds, artichokes, etc., either freeze-dried or artificial. Other adornments include assorted grasses, wheat, salal leaves and bittersweet.

Sherbet Pinwheel Wreath

what you'll need

♦♦♦ AS PLAYFUL AS THE FIRST BREEZE OF SPRING, THE SHERBET PINWHEEL MAKES A LIGHT-

HEARTED DECORATION FOR A CHILD'S BEDROOM, HALLWAY, POWDER ROOM OR

ANYWHERE YOU WANT TO ADD A WHIRL OF COLOR. IT'S SWEET AND SIMPLE

TO CREATE; ONCE YOU TRANSFER THE PATTERN TO YOUR WREATH, IT'S AN

EASY MATTER TO FILL IN WITH DRIFTS OF CANDY TUFT. IT'S LIKE COLORING IN

A COLORING BOOK!

TIME

DIFFICULTY

2 foam wreaths, 12" (30cm) and 8" (20cm)

candy tuft (one bunch each of five spring colors)

Australian daisies

assortment of very narrow (⅛" [3mm] to ¼" [6mm]) satin and sheer ribbons for bow; select colors that coordinate with your candy tuft

raffia

6 yards (5.4m) of inexpensive 1" (2.5cm) ribbon (white)

florist wire

straight pins

florist pins

craft glue

hot glue gun

tweezers

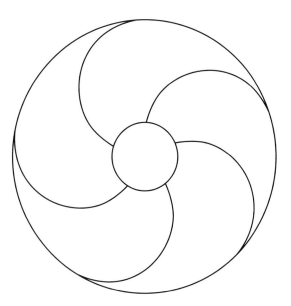

Sherbet Pinwheel Template

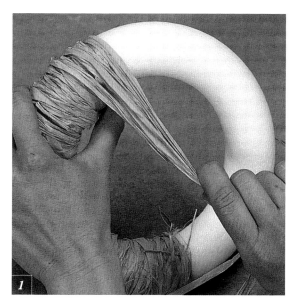

step 1

Raffia-wrap small wreath. Wrap the smaller wreath with raffia as necessary to achieve a good, tight fit inside the larger wreath.

step 2

Double your base. Insert the small wreath flush inside the larger wreath. Glue the seam and wrap with florist wire. Wrap the entire double-form in raffia to achieve a full, even surface to work on.

step 3

Wrap with ribbon. Wrapping your base with one continuous ribbon can be cumbersome, so try cutting your 1" (2.5cm) ribbon into 3-yard (2.7m) lengths. When you come to the end of a ribbon, glue it down, glue the next piece on top and secure both with a straight pin. Keep all your pins on one side of your wreath so you can hide them with the candy tuft.

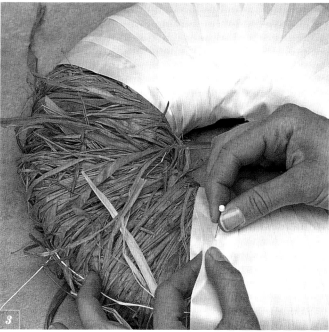

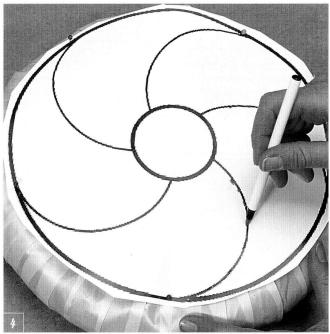

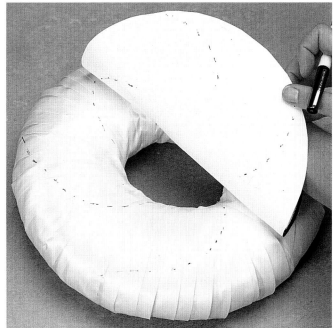

step 4

Transfer the pattern. Enlarge the pattern
from page 40 to approximately 12" (30cm) wide
or the diameter of your prepared base. Transfer
the pattern to the front of your wreath (the side
with the pins), using a sharp-point marker to
poke through the pattern every inch or so. Turn
over and attach a wire for hanging. (see page 11).

step 5

Make bundles of candy tuft. Cut your candy
tuft into small sprigs. Use fine-gauge florist wire
to tie small, single-color bundles about the size
of large grapes.

step 6

Color your pinwheel. Now you're ready to fill
in each section of your pinwheel pattern with a
different color candy tuft! Take a minute to plan
the most pleasing sequence of colors, then grab
your glue gun and fill in one section at a time.
Start from the inside and work your way out, hiding the stems of one bundle behind the head of
the next for a solid, mossy effect. When you're
done, check for any small holes or gaps; fill in
with bits of candy tuft.

step 7

Outline with daisies. Working a couple inches (5cm) at a time, squeeze a thin line of glue between color sections and use tweezers to place Australian daisy heads. Arrange your daisies with a bit of zigzag to give your wreath a little extra personality.

step 8

Add a "confetti" bow. Make a stacked bow with your narrow ribbons (see page 14) and attach with a florist pin.

♦♦♦ The Sherbet Pinwheel Wreath—a real whirl of fun!
As long as you keep your wreath out of direct sunlight, the glorious colors should last a good, long time. If they do fade, try masking each section and perking up with florist spray. Or, better yet, make another Pinwheel Wreath! You can create the same pattern with different effects using caspia, hydrangea, rice flowers, mini roses, Australian daisies and other flowers that are available in an assortment of colors. The method of application will vary depending on the flower.

variation

Design your own
If you're a doodler, have fun creating an original pattern of your very own. I've colored in this swirly design with three shades of globe amaranth.

Keepsake Wreath

what you'll need

♦♦♦ IF (LIKE ME) YOU HAVE DRAWERS AND SHOEBOXES STUFFED WITH SNAPSHOTS, TICKET STUBS, GREETING CARDS AND OTHER RANDOM "TREASURES," THIS WREATH IS FOR YOU! THE KEEPSAKE WREATH OFFERS A PRETTY AND PRACTICAL ALTERNATIVE FOR KEEPING ALL THOSE SPECIAL MEMENTOS TOGETHER IN ONE PLACE. I CREATED THIS ONE FOR MY DAUGH-

TIME

DIFFICULTY

TER'S WEDDING DAY, BUT YOU MIGHT CREATE ONE IN HONOR OF A MILESTONE ANNIVERSARY, A FAMILY REUNION OR A FAVORITE PET. THIS WREATH FEATURES AN INVITATION, A POEM (FRAMED), A ROSETTE FROM THE BRIDE'S SHOE, JEWELRY, GARTER, THE CORK FROM THE COUPLE'S FIRST CHAMPAGNE TOAST, FAVORS, AND EVEN A COUPLE OF COOKIES FROM THE DESSERT TABLE! A TRUE HEIRLOOM TO PASS ON FROM GENERATION TO GENERATION, THE KEEPSAKE WREATH IS A GREAT "SPRING CLEANING" PROJECT TO WORK ON WHILE YOU'RE WAITING FOR YOUR SEEDS TO SPROUT!

14" (36cm) foam base

polyester batting

preserved flowers: 2 small heads of dried hydrangea, 2 stems of spray roses, 3 to 5 rose heads and a few ivy leaves (or substitute your own significant flowers, silk or dried)

10 yards (9m) of 2½" (6.4cm) lace with at least one finished side

8 yards (7m) of narrow (¼" to ¾" [6mm to 19mm]) burgundy ribbon; I used two coordinating ribbons for interest, but you can use the same ribbon if you prefer

3 yards of 1½" (1.3cm) wired ivory satin ribbon for the bow

small framed snapshots and assorted mementos

corsage pins (optional)

florist pins

straight pins

hot glue gun

Preserve Special Occasion Cookies

♦ ♦ ♦ ♦ ♦ ♦ ♦ ♦ ♦ ♦ ♦ ♦ ♦ ♦ ♦ ♦ ♦

Melt paraffin wax. Quickly dip cookie, completely covering in a thin layer of wax. Allow to cool. Repeat.

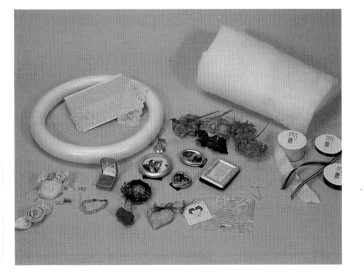

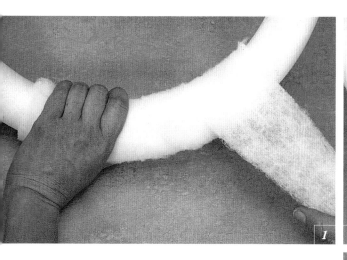

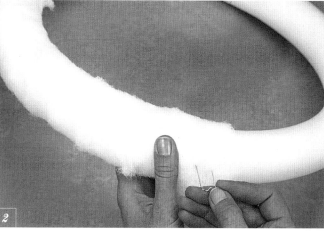

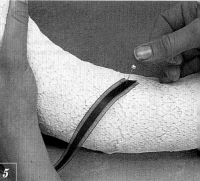

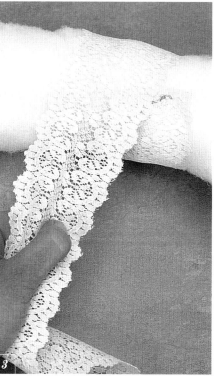

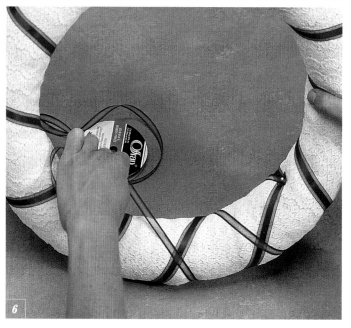

step 1

Wrap base with batting. Cut polyester batting into 3"
(8cm) wide strips. Use a dab of glue and a florist pin to secure the beginning of the first strip to your foam base. Wrap
the strip around your base so it's taught but not tight, keeping
a consistent overlap to achieve a nice, even layer of padding.

step 2

Add more strips. When you come to the end of a strip,
secure it along with the beginning of the next strip using a
dab of hot glue and a florist pin. Continue until your wreath is
completely covered with a generous, even layer of padding.
Go around a second or even a third time, depending on the
look you want to achieve.

step 3

Top with lace. Now cover your padded wreath with one
continuous piece of lace. Begin by securing one end with a
dab of glue and a florist pin.

step 4

Keep an even overlap. Wrap your wreath with the lace,
keeping it taught but not tight and maintaining an even overlap all the way around. When your wreath is completely
covered, secure the end of your lace with a florist pin and attach a wire for hanging (see page 11).

step 5

Spiral with narrow ribbon. Cut a 4-yard (3.6m) length of
narrow ribbon. Pin it to the front of your wreath, near the
point where your lace ends. (Later, you will place your bouquet in this area to hide the rough edges and pinheads.) Spiral the ribbon evenly around your wreath, and pin the end
near the same point you started.

step 6

Crisscross. Repeat with the remaining 4-yard length of narrow ribbon, this time going in the opposite direction to form a
crisscross pattern around the front of your wreath.

◆ MAKING A BOUQUET

step 7
Place one head of hydrangea on top of a stem of spray roses. Secure the stems with a dab of glue.

step 8
Add a rose or two at the base of your hydrangea. Fill in with additional rose heads and ivy leaves as desired. You've just completed half of your bouquet. Repeat the same basic layering—spray rose, hydrangea, rose—to create the second half.

step 9
Place one half of your flower "bouquet" to hide the ends of your lace and narrow ribbons. Secure with hot glue and a straight pin.

step 10
Secure the second half of your bouquet in the same way, leaving 3" to 4" (8cm to 10cm) of space between to attach your bow.

step 11
Make a stacked bow (I made a layered variation—see instructions on page 14) and attach in the center of your bouquet using a piece of fine ribbon.

step 12

Arrange your picture frames. Start by placing your picture frames and other larger mementos in a balanced arrangement around your wreath. Secure them in place using the crisscross ribbons.

step 13

Add mementos. Arrange your mementos around your wreath until you're happy with the spacing and placement. Use either the crisscross ribbons or corsage pins to secure.

♦♦♦ Love and cherish your Keepsake Wreath!

The Keepsake Wreath is intended to be more of a "scrapbook" than a year-round wall decoration. Take it out on anniversaries or whenever you feel like a stroll down memory lane. For the rest of the time, package your wreath with the same love and attention you used to assemble it. Choose a sturdy, generously sized box that opens and closes easily. (Some packaging stores sell boxes specially made for wreaths.) Use acid-free tissue to cushion and protect your wreath, and store it in a low-humidity area. You might even want to cover your box with a pretty wrapping paper!

variation

Oh baby!

For a baby theme, replace the lace with gingham ribbon and fashion the "bow" out of a piece of baby's blanket and a favorite stuffed toy. Attach booties, birth announcement, silver cup and other sweet little mementos of babyhood.

Summer Glory >

♦♦♦ Summer erupts. Greens so green they almost hurt the eyes…glorious riots of butterflies and blooms…childhood memories floating on the breeze. A person could just sit all summer long and take it in. But of course there are flowers to water, weeds to pull and wreaths to make!

This is the time to gather and dry peonies, roses, hydrangea, daisies and other favorite flowers. (Be sure to dry enough to see you through the winter!) Keep your eyes open for little pinwheels, pretty seed packets, interesting twigs, mosses and other unique additions for your wreaths. Add sweet hints of summer with aromas of rose, heather, peach, apple and vanilla.

On the following pages, you'll find wreaths to dress up picnics and terra cotta pots, wreaths inspired by garden views and strolls along the seashore, plus a quick and easy star-shaped wreath that will brighten your summers for years to come.

(above) TERRA COTTA POT-TOPPER; (opposite page starting from upper left, clockwise) LILAC PICNIC CHANDELIER, GARDEN VIEW WREATH, AMERI-CANA WREATH, SEASIDE WREATH

Lilac Picnic Chandelier

what you'll need

♦♦♦ THERE IS NOTHING MORE ROMANTIC THAN A SUMMER PICNIC—ESPECIALLY WHEN SERVED BENEATH THIS CHANDELIER WREATH AT DUSK. ASIDE FROM BEING AN ENCHANTING GARDEN DECORATION, THE LILAC PICNIC CHANDELIER OFFERS A WONDERFUL USE FOR A GLASS CLOCHE AFTER IT HAS SERVED ITS PURPOSE OF NURTURING SPRING SEEDLINGS. IN KEEPING WITH THE EASY-GOING SPIRIT OF PICNIC ENTERTAINING, THIS WREATH IS FUN AND SIMPLE TO CREATE. IT'S BEST WHEN SERVED WITH ONE LOADED PICNIC BASKET, A NICE, SOFT BLANKET (PREFERABLY RED GINGHAM) AND A PERFECT SUMMER DAY.

TIME

DIFFICULTY

metal ring ; I used a 10" (25cm) ring, but you should choose the size that supports your cloche

natural raffia

4 slip rings and 1 S-hook

60" (152cm) of fine chain, cut into 3 equal pieces

6 silk lilacs

silk hydrangeas with leaves (4 white, 2 green)

stem of green berries

6 yards (5.4m) of ½" to 1" (1.3cm to 2.5cm) sheer ribbon for bows

glass cloche or garden bell

florist wire

hot glue gun

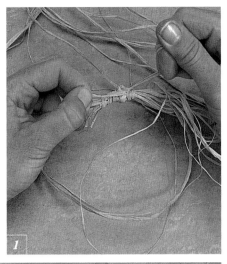

step 1

Attach raffia to ring. Take a few strands of raffia and knot an end onto your metal ring. Secure with a dab of hot glue and allow to dry.

step 2

Wrap. Wrap the raffia tightly around the ring, making sure no metal shows through. Add new strands of raffia as needed; overlap the end of a strand with the beginning of a new strand, secure with a dab of glue, and bind tightly with a single piece of raffia.

step 3

Attach slip rings. Attach three of the slip rings, evenly spacing them around the metal ring.

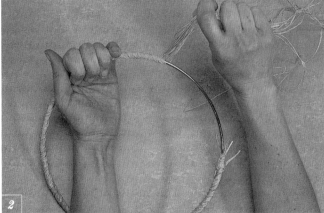

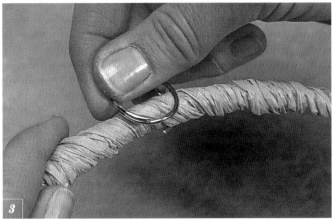

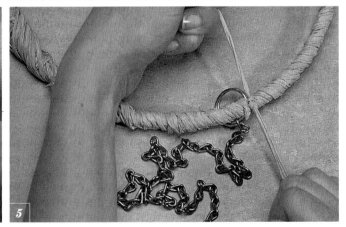

step 4

Add chain. Attach a length of 20" (51cm) chain to each slip ring.

step 5

Secure hoops. Use a piece of raffia to tie each slip ring in place, being sure to keep all three knots on the same side of the ring. This will be the bottom of your chandelier. Trim excess raffia.

step 6

Glue in place. Add a dab of hot glue to ensure the hoops won't budge.

step 7

Complete the hanging chain. Slip the top of all three chains onto the fourth slip ring. (Be sure to slip them on in order to ensure your chandelier hangs level.) Through the completion of your wreath, let the chain hang down through the center of your wreath to keep it out of the way.

step 8

Start with your lilacs. Wire on your lilacs to hang down evenly around the hoop. (Remember, the hanging chain indicates the top of your chandelier, so make sure you're hanging your lilacs in the right direction. And be careful not to wire up your chain as you go!)

step 9

Top with white hydrangea. Cut the leaves off your hydrangeas and set aside; you'll be using some of them in step 11. Cut your white hydrangea into florets. Use florist wire to fill in the top of your hoop with the hydrangea.

step 10

Fill in with green hydrangea. Now cut the green hydrangea into florets. Use florist wire to intersperse them among the white hydrangea, filling in any thin spots.

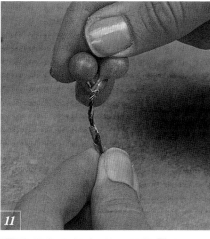

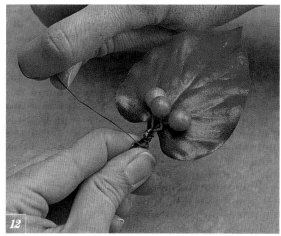

step 11
Make berry clusters. "Harvest" your berry stem by pulling or cutting off each berry, being sure to leave a stem of wire. Twist together into groups of three.

step 12
Make berry picks. Wire each berry cluster to the base of a hydrangea leaf.

step 13
Camouflage stems. Wrap berry wires and leaf stem with green florist tape.

step 14
Attach berry picks. Use your glue gun to intersperse the berry picks randomly among the hydrangea.

step 15
Finish with bows. Make three stacked bows (see page 14) and attach to the base of each hanging chain.

♦♦♦ **Feast your eyes on your finished Lilac Picnic Chandelier!** Use the S-hook to suspend your Lilac Picnic Chandelier from a favorite tree. Then simply anchor a candle in your cloche using white sand or salt, and carefully slip it into the wreath. All that's left to do now is pack up the picnic basket! If you'd like to use a chandelier wreath as an indoor accent—suspended in a bay window, perhaps—consider creating a dried version using globe amaranth, rose buds, yarrow and other durable flowers.

variation

Tabletop wreath
Start by cutting a circle of 2" (5cm) thick foam large enough to anchor your cloche and serve as the base of your wreath. Remove a small circle of foam from the center to fit snuggly around the knob of your cloche, then press the cloche firmly down into the base to embed. Build your wreath directly on the foam. (I used peonies, love-lies-bleeding and other dried flowers.)

Seaside Wreath

what you'll need

♦♦♦ TWO OF MY FRIENDS RETURNED FROM A FUN-FILLED TRIP TO ARUBA WITH THE LOVELY
SEASHELLS THAT INSPIRED THIS WREATH. IT'S SWIMMING WITH WHIMSICAL STARFISH AND AN
ASSORTMENT OF OCEAN-HUED DRIED MATERIALS—GLOBE THISTLE "URCHINS," TING TING
"SEAWEED," WAVES OF CASPIA AND GYPSY GRASS. ALL THAT'S MISSING IS THE SAND

TIME

BETWEEN YOUR TOES! I MADE A SEASIDE WREATH FOR EACH OF MY FRIENDS—

DIFFICULTY

ONE WITH DRIED FLOWERS AND ONE WITH SILK (SEE PAGE 63). IT'S NO TICKET
TO ARUBA, BUT I HOPE IT SERVES AS A LASTING, YEAR-ROUND REMINDER OF THE
WONDERFUL TIME THEY HAD THERE.

14" (36cm) grapevine wreath

caspia in two shades of blue

gyspy grass, whitewashed blue

hydrangea, 3 heads green and
2 heads blue

assortment of blue dried flowers—
everlastings, globe thistle, baby
everlastings, sea holly, eucalyptus

ting ting, green

maidenhair fern

small piece of driftwood,
about 10" (25cm) long

starfish—1 large, 3 medium
and various small ones

assorted seashells

10 yards (9m) of ⅛" (3mm)
blue satin ribbon

florist wire

hot glue gun

Substitute Your Favorites

♦ ♦ ♦ ♦ ♦ ♦ ♦ ♦ ♦ ♦ ♦ ♦ ♦ ♦

You can make this wreath as simple
or elaborate as you like. Take a stroll
down the dried-flower aisle of your
neighborhood craft store and pick out
any sea-worthy elements you find,
such as German statice, frosted mint,
diamond eucalyptus, lepto, nigella,
poppy pods, scabiosa, springerii fern,
curly willow and veronica.

step 1

Secure the driftwood. Position the driftwood along the bottom of your wreath. Use a piece of florist wire to secure each end. Turn your wreath over and attach wire for hanging (see page 11).

step 2

Begin building your background. Make small, mixed bundles of the lighter caspia and gypsy grass. Use these bundles to cover the inside and outside edges of the top half of your wreath.

step 3

Fill in with hydrangea. Use pieces of green hydrangea to fill in between caspia/gypsy grass bundles on the top half of your wreath. (See page 13 for special tips on working with hydrangea.)

step 4

Get darker and keep going. Repeat steps 2 and 3 to cover the bottom half of your wreath, this time using darker caspia in the gypsy grass bundles and blue hydrangea to fill in between. Use these flowers to help camouflage the wire securing your driftwood. Now you have a rich, variegated background on which to "paint" your ocean scene!

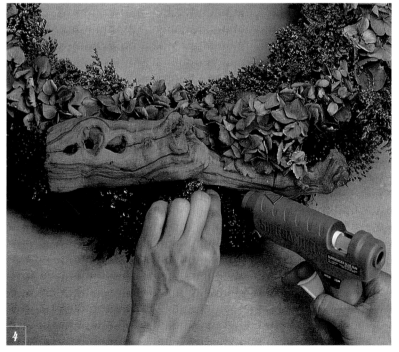

step 5

Start with your "star" fish. Place your largest starfish on one side of your wreath, establishing your focal point. Work in your larger shells and starfish, concentrating them on the bottom, or the "ocean floor" of your wreath. Once you're happy with the arrangement, glue into place.

step 6

Add everlastings and globe thistle. Glue these randomly around your wreath.

step 7

And now for the little touches. Intersperse sprigs of sea holly and small bundles of baby everlastings around the top half of your wreath. Add some small shells and starfish around the entire wreath. (For an extra touch of fun, use two small shells and a small faux pearl to create a treasure-filled oyster!)

step 8

Create starfish burst. Bring more focus to your large starfish with a burst of eucalyptus, ting ting and maidenhair fern. Place a few stems of each radiating out from the top of your starfish, angled out slightly from your wreath for added dimension. Use a dab of glue at the base of each stem to secure.

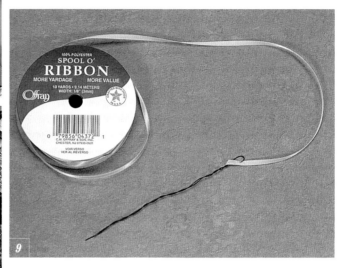

step 9

Thread your "needle". Cut a small slit at the end of your narrow ribbon. Thread a 6" (15cm) length of florist wire through the slit, bend the wire in half and twist. This is your ribbon-weaving needle.

step 10

Make "ripples" of ribbon. Pass your ribbon under and around flowers, in essence weaving your ribbon into your wreath. Aim for random but even coverage all around your wreath.

♦♦♦ Splash into summer with your completed Seaside Wreath! The Seaside Wreath is at home in the bedroom, family room, home office (for quality daydreaming!) and even the bathroom, as long as it's not exposed to a lot of steam. (Otherwise, consider making a silk version.) If the ocean isn't your idea of a dream vacation, how about making a Mountain Wreath with an earthy assortment of dried mosses, pinecones and leaves?

variation

Swimming in silks
You can create a stunning seaside wreath using silk materials—a much more durable option if you intend to display your wreath in a bathroom. Add a few fish, seashells and some coral pieces to complete your silk seascape.

Americana Wreath

what you'll need

◆◆◆ DON'T YOU LOVE THE SIMPLE THINGS IN LIFE? TAKE THIS WREATH, FOR EXAMPLE. BIND SOME BRANCHES TOGETHER, TOSS IN A ROSE, TIE ON A BOW AND THERE YOU HAVE IT—THE PERFECT PATRIOTIC TOUCH FOR THE FOURTH OF JULY! FOLLOW A FEW SIMPLE STEPS TO PREPARE YOUR BIRCH (OR TO MAKE ANY TYPE OF WOOD LOOK LIKE BIRCH!), AND THE NATURAL BEAUTY OF THIS STAR WILL SHINE ON LONG AFTER THE FRESH ROSE FADES. FUN AND FOLKSY, THE AMERICANA WREATH IS AT HOME INSIDE OR OUT, ON SCREEN DOOR OR GARDEN GATE. I LIKE MINE ON THE GARDEN SHED!

TIME

DIFFICULTY

5 relatively straight branches of roughly the same length (20" [51cm]) and diameter (1" [2.5cm]); I prefer white birch, but any wood will do

1 fresh red rose

3 yards of 1" (2.5cm) blue wired ribbon for bow

coping saw

sanding block or sandpaper

white gesso

acrylic spray

twine

strip of plastic (I cut mine from a milk jug)

2 slip rings

florist water tube

florist wire

hot glue gun

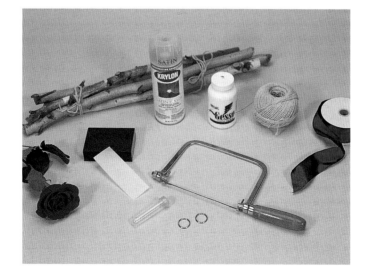

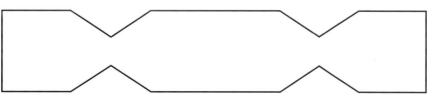

Template for flower tube holder

Prepare Your Birch

◆ ◆

We think of birch as being pretty white, but chances are the branches you find will look a little dingy. So here's an easy way to brighten and protect them:

1. **SAND** ◆ Start by using a sanding block or sandpaper to remove any dirt and loose bark from your branches.

2. **PAINT** ◆ Brush each branch with gesso, avoiding the ends to allow the natural wood to show.

3. **WIPE** ◆ Use a paper towel or rag to wipe off enough gesso to achieve a white-washed effect. Allow to dry.

4. **DE-NUB** ◆ Cut off any "nubs" to expose spots of natural wood. If you painted over any of the ends of your branches, cut off a thin slice to expose the natural wood.

5. **SEAL** ◆ Spray branches with acrylic spray and allow to dry. This will protect the finish and give it a pretty, transparent shine. Now your branches look like the bright, white birch we all know and love! And they'll stay that way.

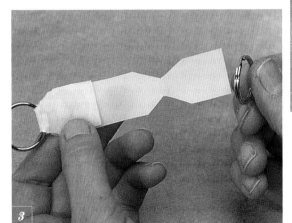

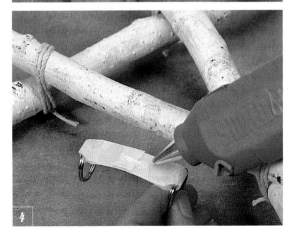

step 1

Arrange your star. Arrange your branches into a star shape. Every branch is shaped a little differently, so take a few minutes to experiment and find the best fit.

step 2

Tie the joints. Tie the branches together at each intersection with a piece of twine. Secure with a simple square knot and trim ends. Attach a wire hoop at the top point for hanging (See page 11).

step 3

Make a flower tube holder. Cut a strip of plastic using the template on page 65. Slip on the slip rings to rest in the notches. Fold over the plastic and secure with dab of hot glue.

step 4

Attach the tube holder to the wreath. Squeeze a strip of glue on the back of your tube holder and glue in place.

step 5

Add one red rose. Trim the stem as necessary and insert it into the tube, allowing the birch to support the rose.

step 6

Add bow. Make a stacked bow (see page 14) and attach with florist wire.

◆◆◆ A Star is Born!

For a less patriotic theme, choose a different color for your bow, replace the red rose with a sunflower or zinnia, or skip the flower altogether. The simple beauty of this birch star is bright enough to stand on its own. And best of all, you made it with plenty of time left over to relax and enjoy a nice, icy glass of tea. Mmm, gotta love those simple things!

variation

Window to winter

Birch is such a great material to work with—especially if you can get it free from your backyard. Using three pieces per side, I made this dimensional rectangle and decorated it with twisted wisteria vines, juniper, pepperberries and frosted canella berries.

Garden View Wreath

what you'll need

♦♦♦ THIS IS MY FAVORITE WREATH TO GIVE AS A GIFT BECAUSE IT IS SO OPEN TO PERSONAL-IZATION. CHOOSE COLORS, FLOWERS AND ACCESSORIES WITH THE RECIPIENT IN MIND. YOU COULD EVEN INCLUDE THEIR NAME ON A RUSTIC LITTLE SIGN: "LAURIE'S GARDEN" OR "WELCOME TO KIRK'S WOODS" OR "JAMIE WEEDS HERE!" CRAFT STORES OFFER ALL KINDS OF FUN

TIME

DIFFICULTY

MINIATURE ACCESSORIES TO BRING YOUR SCENE TO LIFE—GARDEN BENCHES, BUNNIES, WIND CHIMES, BICYCLES, CROQUET SETS, TIRE SWINGS, YOU NAME IT! LITTLE DETAILS LIKE THESE INVITE PEOPLE TO LEAN IN AND LOOK CLOSER. SO—ARE YOU READY TO GET "PLANTING"?

18" (46cm) straw wreath; I like straw wreaths because they offer a nice, wide surface to work on, but if weight is an issue, you can substitute a foam base

2-3 heads assorted hydrangea

assorted dried flowers—I used German statice, caspia, sweet Annie, candy tuft, Australian daisies, rice flowers and sanfordii

sheet moss

reindeer moss

preserved boxwood

2-3 small sponge mushrooms

3-4 small, thin river rocks

15" (38cm) tree branch (look for one that's forked at one end)

two 4½" (12cm) lengths of ½" (1.3cm) dowel rod

twig fence

a variety of miniature accessories— I used a watering can, terra cotta pots, wheelbarrow, old-fashioned reel mower, straw hat, welcome sign, vegetables, beehive and bees, birds, bird's nest and eggs, unpainted birdhouse, garden tools, and, for my gazing ball, a tiny glass bauble and an unfinished pedestal

acrylic paints

florist pins

florist wire

fishing line or twine

hot glue gun

Other Ideas for Mini Flower Gardens

♦ ♦ ♦ ♦ ♦ ♦ ♦ ♦ ♦ ♦ ♦

silver sage ♦ red cedar ♦ veronica ♦ larkspur ♦ gypsophilia ♦ flowering oregano ♦ pepperberries ♦ lepto ♦ dudinea ♦ baby's breath ♦ beech

step 1

Start with a moss background. Dampen moss and cover the entire wreath, securing well using glue, florist pins and wire. Attach a wire for hanging on the back (see page 11). Make sure your hanging wire is a secure one—this wreath has some weight to it.

step 2

Place mushroom ledges and stepping stones. Glue in your sponge mushrooms, clustered to one side of your wreath. Starting on the opposite side, stagger your river rock stepping stones to lead toward the center of the wreath where you'll place your gate. Use florist pins underneath as needed for added support. (You'll camouflage the pins later.) Now you have little "ledges" for displaying your miniature decorations!

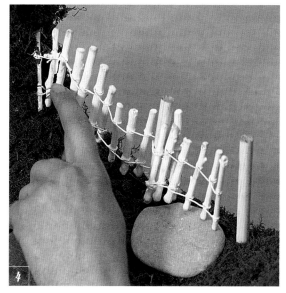

step 3

Plant the tree and fence posts. Place your "tree trunk," trimming it as necessary to fit. Glue into place and hold firmly against your wreath for a few minutes while the glue dries to ensure a tight bond. Sharpen one end of each piece of dowel (a pencil sharpener works great for this!), squeeze a dab of glue onto each point, and insert into straw to mark the placement of your gate.

step 4

Place the fence. Use florist pins and glue to secure the outer ends onto the wreath. Glue the inner ends to the dowel posts, leaving a couple of inches (5cm) of overlap on one side to form your gate.

step 5
Add foliage. Glue boxwood "branches" onto your tree.

step 6
Plant hydrangea shrubs. Break hydrangea heads into smaller pieces, and glue down the opposite side of your wreath. (See page 13 for special tips on working with hydrangea.)

step 7
Add tree blossoms. Now that you have your foundation built, it's time for the details! First, glue small sprigs of German statice into your boxwood branches.

step 8
Plant your flower garden. Snuggle the beehive into place among the hydrangea. Next, make small bundles of each of your assorted flowers. Start gluing these in under your hydrangea and work your way down.

step 9
Add some shrubbery. Glue a little shrubbery alongside your tree trunk. Here, I've used a few sprigs of yellow caspia and sanfordii.

step 10
Fill your flower pots. Glue a tiny bit of moss into the bottom of each mini terra cotta pot. Fill with tiny bundles of assorted flowers.

step 11

Make your gazing ball. Paint your pedestal base gray to look like stone. When it's dry, glue your bauble on top. Voila! A gazing ball! (I bet, with a little thought, you can come up with your own clever tricks for creating original garden accessories!)

step 12

Load your wheelbarrow. Glue larger veggies on bottom and smaller on top.

step 13

Accessorize. Now for the really fun part! Fill your bird's nest with eggs and nestle among the tree branches. Perch a birdie on the fence post. Glue your welcome sign to the tree. Park your wheelbarrow on the ledge and lean your garden tools against the tree. Arrange your flower pots and other accessories on your stepping stones. Buzz a few bees around the hive.

step 14

Hang birdhouse. Use acrylic paints to decorate your birdhouse and allow to dry. Suspend from a tree branch using fishing line or twine.

step 15

Touch up with moss. Glue small tufts of reindeer moss under stones and ledges, at base of flower garden, or wherever you need to soften rough edges and hide florist pins.

✦✦✦ **Take a minute to sit and enjoy your Garden View!**
Wasn't that fun? Now any room in your home can have a picturesque view! (Just be extra careful to use a secure hook or nail to hang this one, as it has some weight to it.) Don't forget to keep your eyes open for fun little additions to use in your next Garden View. Let your imagination loose, and every scene you create will be a true original!

variation

Get even more detailed
I made this wreath in memory of our dear neighbor Bob, an avid gardener. The arbor is a piece of wire covered with dried morning glory vines and mini rosebuds. I made the fence from balsa wood. The apples are unfinished mini apples I purchased from a craft store and dyed red. The wall is fashioned from real stone glued onto a piece of foam.

Terra Cotta Pot Topper

what you'll need

♦♦♦ THERE'S SOMETHING SWEET AND OLD-FASHIONED ABOUT GIVING GIFTS FROM THE GARDEN. AND I NEVER MET AN HERB GARDENER WHO WASN'T HAPPY TO DISCOVER A NEW USE FOR HIS EVER-ABUNDANT HARVEST! THE TERRA COTTA POT TOPPER IS QUICK AND EASY TO PUT TOGETHER—ESPECIALLY IF YOU MAKE THE CHICKEN-WIRE BASE AHEAD OF

TIME

DIFFICULTY

TIME. (YOU MAY EVEN WANT TO MAKE A FEW, JUST TO HAVE ON HAND!) ADORN WITH HANDFULS OF FRESH-CUT HERBS (SMELLS WONDERFUL!), ADD SOME BERRIES (I USE FREEZE-DRIED, BUT FRESH WILL WORK JUST AS WELL) AND FINISH WITH FRESH SUNFLOWERS, DAISIES, ZINNIAS OR WHATEVER'S BLOOMING IN YOUR BACK-YARD. BY ITSELF OR FILLED WITH GOODIES, THE TERRA COTTA POT TOPPER MAKES A UNIQUE AND NEIGHBORLY GIFT.

piece of chicken wire at least 36" x 6" (91cm x 15cm)

floral moss

8" (20cm) terra cotta pot

fresh herbs (I used marjoram, oregano, sage, dill, thyme and chives)

freeze-dried berries (18 strawberries and 9 blackberries)

3 fresh mini sunflower heads

2 yards (1.8m) of ½" (12mm) gingham ribbon

natural raffia

copper plant tag

florist wire

green florist tape

hot glue gun

Wreathmaker's Garden

♦ ♦ ♦ ♦ ♦ ♦ ♦ ♦ ♦ ♦ ♦ ♦ ♦

In addition to beautifying your landscape, these plants yield foliage, berries, vines and other materials you can use in your wreaths all year round.
arborvitae ♦ birches ♦ bittersweet ♦ boxwood ♦ crabapple ♦ English ivy ♦ fountain grasses ♦ grapes ♦ hydrangea ♦ junipers ♦ lilacs ♦ maple ♦ morning glory ♦ mosses ♦ oaks ♦ pines ♦ pussy willow ♦ pyracantha ♦ roses ♦ spruces ♦ wisteria ♦ yews ♦ and don't forget assorted herbs and flowers!

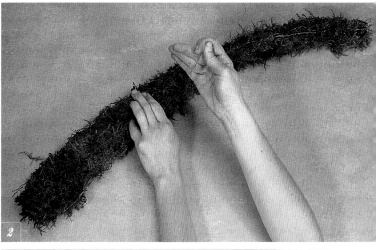

step 1

Make a moss-filled tube. Cut a piece of chicken wire about 36" x 6" (91cm x 15cm). Place a strip of damp moss along the center and form the wire into a tube. (Soaking your moss in water beforehand will help keep the herbs and flowers fresh a little longer. Squeeze out excess water before using.)

step 2

Sew it up. Use florist wire to sew together the seam of your tube. (Careful of sharp edges!)

step 3

Top your pot. Wrap the tube around your pot, molding the chicken wire to hug the top edge. Use florist wire to connect the ends of the tube.

step 4

Add chives. Gather three bunches of chives. Arrange evenly around the top of your wreath, leaving a few inches of overhang on the ends. Use florist wire to tack each chive bunch to the chicken wire in two or three places.

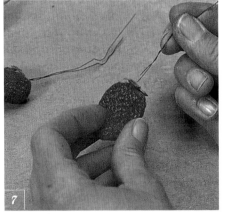

step 5

Add herb bundles. Make two bundles of assorted herbs. Using a long piece of raffia, join them—stem to stem—to form one double-ended bundle. Use the raffia to tie the bundle to the chicken wire, centered above a bunch of chives. Top the other two chive bunches the same way.

step 6

Add raffia bows. Now for a little touch of raffia. Attach a small, simple bow to the center of each herb bundle.

step 7

Wire strawberries. Cut 8" (20cm) wires, bend in half, and insert into your strawberries. Use a dab of hot glue to secure. Allow to dry.

step 8

Bundle strawberries. Make six bundles, each with three strawberries and a small bunch of herbs. Twist together the strawberry wires to secure. If necessary, wrap each stem with green florist tape to camouflage.

step 9

Add strawberries. Space the strawberry bundles evenly around your wreath, bending each wire stem to "hook" into the chicken wire.

step 10

Add blackberries. Wire the blackberries the same as you did the strawberries. Twist together three clusters of three berries each, and wrap each stem with green florist tape to camouflage. Use the stems to hook the berry trios under each raffia bow.

step 11

Add sunflowers. Cut the stem of each sunflower about 3" (8cm) long. Using needlenose pliers or some other handy hole-poking tool, make three holes evenly spaced around the top of your wreath. Insert flowers, securing with florist wire if necessary.

step 12

Final touches. Make three simple gingham bows and attach under each sunflower. Tie the plant tag on with one of these bows to use as a gift tag.

♦♦♦**Add a dash of kindness to someone's day with your completed Terra Cotta Pot Topper!** Fill your pot with goodies (seeds, gloves, tools, lotion, etc.) and present to your favorite gardening friend. She's sure to appreciate the thought as well as the herbs, which will dry naturally and can be pinched off and used for cooking. No need to limit your "toppers" to terra cotta pots. For a get-well gift, present a jar of homemade chicken soup with a mini topper of lavender. For a cat lover, top a ceramic water bowl with fresh catnip and little kitty toys. Top a pail, a basket, a watering can with dried flowers, silk flowers, "found" art…oh, the top-abilities!

variation

Baker's gift wreath

Here's a sweet-smelling wreath you can make for a friend who likes to bake. Form a chicken-wire base on the rim of a pretty mixing bowl and wrap with cheesecloth to soften. Create a pattern using star anise, whole nutmeg, allspice and bay leaves. Tie on gingham bows, cinnamon sticks and cookie cutters, then fill with baking goodies.

Fall Homecoming

◆◆◆ My idea of perfection is a fall day. I never feel more at home on this earth than I do on a crisp autumn afternoon, surrounded by the crescendo of colorful leaves, kaleidoscope skies, fields of gold and the familiar smell of wood burning in the air. Inside, the house is filled with the comforting smells of cinnamon and apple pie, of cloves, mulberry and spices. It all makes you want to slow down, sit back and breathe deeply.

The wreaths in this chapter celebrate the season with colorful leaves, acorns, goldenrod, berries, cornhusk, grapevines, gourds, citrus peels and other autumn treasures. The palette ranges from the earthy tones of the Country Roads Wreath to the vibrant golds and reds of Fall Bounty. Whether you prefer the rustic style of Cornhusk & Curls, the casual elegance of the Pumpkin Garland, or the fresh and edible Cornucopia Dessert Wreath, these projects will welcome the warm pleasures of fall into your home.

(above) PUMPKIN GARLAND; (opposite page starting from upper left, clockwise) FALL BOUNTY, CORNUCOPIA DESSERT WREATH, CORNHUSK & CURLS, COUNTRY ROADS WREATH

Fall Bounty Wreath

what you'll need

♦♦♦ THIS WREATH CELEBRATES THE FULL GLORY OF FALL IN A RAGE OF SILK FLOWERS, VELVET

LEAVES, BEADED BERRIES AND RIBBONS. YOU WOULDN'T GUESS TO LOOK AT IT, BUT

TIME

THIS WREATH IS ACTUALLY INEXPENSIVE AND FAIRLY SIMPLE TO ASSEMBLE. YOU

DIFFICULTY

COULD EASILY MAKE A SMALLER VERSION FOR HALF THE PRICE—EVEN LESS

IF YOU KEEP YOUR EYES OPEN FOR SILK FLOWER SALES AND BARGAINS. IF YOU'RE

GOING TO SPLURGE, SAVE IT FOR THE FOCAL FLOWERS.

2 straw wreaths, 18" (46cm)
and 24" (61cm)

4-6 inexpensive bunches of
assorted silk mums with leaves
(about 60 medium and large
heads in coordinating fall colors)

grapevine, about 35" (89cm) long,
ideally with a split

4-5 stems of assorted small silk
filler flowers (such as stock or
straw flowers)

1-2 stems of "focal" silk flowers
(I used ranunculus)

1-2 stems of silk Japanese lanterns

2 bunches of velvet leaves
(about 30 leaves)

two 5-yard (4.5m) lengths of
1½" (3.8cm) wired ribbon
in coordinating fall colors

2-3 stems of artificial berries

10 beaded berry picks

florist wire

florist pins

hot glue gun

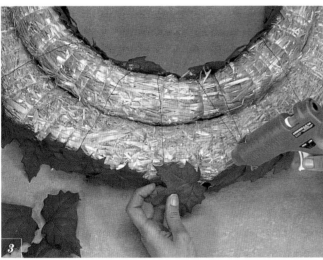

step 1

Build the double-decker base. Center the smaller wreath on top of the larger one. (No need to press flush—tiering will give the wreath added dimension.) Glue along the seam and wrap with wire to secure. This nice wide base is the hidden secret behind this wreath's full, lush look. Attach wire for hanging (see page 11).

step 2

Clip your flowers. "Harvest" your mum bunches, clipping off individual flowers, leaving 2" to 3" (5cm to 8cm) stems.

step 3

Camouflage your straw base. Using the leaves you just clipped off, cover the inner and outer edges of your wreath. Overlap the leaves slightly as needed for a solid, uniform coverage. This will hide any straw that may show around the flowers, giving your wreath a nice, finished look.

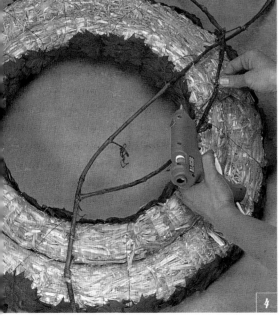

step 4

Secure the grapevine. Place your grapevine across the bottom half of your wreath. Pin and glue on each side to secure.

step 5

Biggest flowers first. Use your largest mums to form your base layer. It's a good idea to first place the flowers (poke the stems right into the straw) and then—once you're sure they are distributed evenly around your wreath—go back and glue into place. (This way you won't run out of flowers when you're 90 percent done!) This first layer of flowers should sit flush against your wreath.

step 6

Next layer: smaller mums. Again, it's a good idea to place all your smaller mums first, then go back and glue in place. Vary the height of this layer of flowers to add depth, nestling some among the larger mums and allowing others to sit slightly higher.

step 7

Work in your filler flowers. Cut your filler flowers into small sprigs and arrange around your wreath as desired. I like to concentrate mine around the grapevine.

step 8

Add the Japanese lanterns. Cut your Japanese lanterns into small pieces—clusters of three or five pods—and arrange as desired around your wreath.

step 9

Add velvet leaves. Cut your velvet bunches into individual leaves and glue around your wreath as desired. For fun, glue one or two "tumbling" across your grapevine.

step 10

Weave in ribbon. Work one of your ribbons through the wreath, weaving under and around the flowers, tacking down with florist pins as needed. Repeat with second ribbon. Aim for a relatively even coverage over the entire wreath.

step 11

Add berries. Cut your berry sprays into small sprigs. Distribute these sprigs along with your berry picks around your wreath as desired and glue into place.

step 12

Finish with your "focal" flowers. For the final touch, cut your focal flowers down to stems of 2" to 3" (5cm to 8cm), concentrate them within one quadrant of your wreath and glue into place.

♦♦♦ A brilliant burst of fall!
This wreath is worthy of a featured spot over a fireplace or on a sheltered front door. You'll be sorry when it's time to pack it away for the winter. The good news is that you can use the same techniques to create a "bountiful" silk wreath for any season!

variation

Spring fling!
Add a blast of spring to any room with assorted silk flowers. Have fun incorporating butterflies, ladybugs or other little camouflaged surprises.

Pumpkin Garland

♦♦♦ HALLOWEEN JUST WOULDN'T BE HALLOWEEN WITHOUT PUMPKINS! IF YOU'RE IN THE MOOD FOR A MORE ELEGANT ALTERNATIVE TO THE TRADITIONAL JACK-O-LANTERN, I HAVE JUST THE THING. THE PUMPKIN GARLAND IS A GREAT WAY TO USE THOSE PRETTY, BEADED GRAPES THAT ARE SO POPULAR THESE DAYS. IT'S WHAT ALL THE BEST-DRESSED PUMPKINS WILL BE WEARING THIS FALL! AND BEST OF ALL, IT'S SUPER SIMPLE TO MAKE—THE HARDEST PART WILL BE CHOOSING YOUR FAVORITE PUMPKIN.

TIME

DIFFICULTY

a few wisteria vines; instead of wisteria, you can use a metal hoop wrapped in raffia (see page 54)

3 bunches of beaded grapes, velvet grapes or beaded berries

1 large head of dried green hydrangea

3 yards (2.7m) of 1½" (3.8cm) wide wired green silk ribbon for bows

12 velvet ivy leaves

light-gauge, green cloth-covered stem wire for tendrils

pumpkin

florist wire

hot glue gun

Before You Start

♦ ♦ ♦ ♦ ♦ ♦ ♦ ♦ ♦ ♦ ♦ ♦ ♦ ♦ ♦

Soak wisteria in water for one hour or, better yet, overnight. This makes it much more flexible and easier to work with.

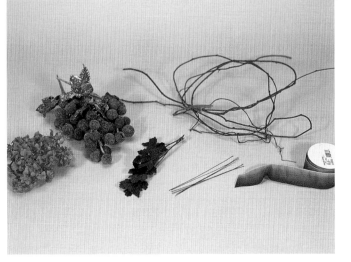

step 1
Make a custom-fit wreath. Start by forming a wreath of wisteria about halfway down your pumpkin. Twist the wisteria around itself, adding vines until you achieve the width desired and the wreath sits about an inch lower than where you'd ultimately like it. (This will allow for the shrinkage that occurs as the wreath dries.) Allow the wreath to dry overnight.

step 2
Add grapes. Wire on the grape bunches, evenly spaced around your wreath.

step 3
Add hydrangea. Break the hydrangea into pieces and use it to fill in around grape clusters, leaving space between to add bows. (See page 13 for special tips on working with hydrangea.)

step 4
Add bows. Make three small stacked bows (see page 14) and wire on between the grape clusters.

step 5
Add velvet leaves. Squeeze a dab of glue onto each stem, and slip in velvet leaves here and there around your wreath.

step 6
Add "tendrils". Using the end of a paintbrush or similar form, curl wires around and around to make curlicues. Glue the tendrils here and there around your wreath as desired.

♦♦♦ **What a treat!**
It's that easy to turn an ordinary
pumpkin into a festive centerpiece,
and the average jack-o-lantern into
a Greek gourdish god! Make several
garland-topped pumpkins to create
a dramatic grouping for your table,
kitchen counter or stairway. When
your pumpkin is past its peak, you
can still use your garland around
the base of a hurricane.

variation

A basket case
Give a favorite basket the same special treatment. I used a
metal hoop wrapped in raffia for the base of this wreath. If
needed, use S-hooks to suspend your finished wreath from
the rim of your basket.

Country Roads Wreath

what you'll need

♦♦♦ THE MAKINGS FOR THIS ALL-NATURAL WREATH CAME FROM THE BACKROADS OF INDIANA COUNTY, PENNSYLVANIA—MY VERY OWN "WEED GARDEN!" GRAB YOUR PRUNERS AND HEAD OUT TO A QUIET COUNTRY LANE OR MEADOW WHEN THE WEEDS AND WILDFLOWERS START COMING INTO BLOOM (IN MY NECK OF THE WOODS IT'S AROUND JUNE). EARLY FALL IS THE BEST TIME FOR HARVESTING GOLDENROD—TRY TO GET IT JUST BEFORE ITS PRIME, WHEN IT'S NICE AND GOLDEN. FALL IS ALSO THE TIME TO GATHER THISTLES, MILKWEED PODS, ROSE HIPS AND, OF COURSE, ALL THOSE GORGEOUS LEAVES. DON'T WORRY ABOUT FINDING THE EXACT MATERIALS SHOWN HERE. USE THE PLANTS NATIVE TO YOUR AREA AND YOUR WREATH IS GUARANTEED TO BE A TRUE ORIGINAL.

TIME

DIFFICULTY

oval grapevine base—mine is about 15" x 30" (38cm x 76cm)

dried goldenrod

assortment of air-dried flowers, wild grasses and berries (I used black-eyed Susans, crown of corn, millet, milkweed pods, wild roses, elderberries, bittersweet, sunflowers and thistles sprayed burgundy for extra contrast)

Queen Anne's lace (preserved in silica gel)

assortment of preserved fall leaves (purchase in craft store or make your own by following the simple instructions on this page)

curly gold raffia

acrylic spray

florist wire

hot glue gun

Preserving Autumn Leaves

1. START WITH LEAVES that are unblemished, intact and colorful. The colors will darken slightly, so be sure to start with the brightest leaves you can find.

2. WORKING ON AN IRONING BOARD or a cotton towel topped with newspaper, sandwich your leaf between two sheets of wax paper. Make sure the leaf is nice and flat. Slip the wax paper between two paper towels.

3. WITH A DRY IRON on low to medium setting, press your leaf "sandwich." The heat will soften the wax paper, lightly coating and preserving the leaf in wax. (Use fresh wax paper for each leaf. The paper towels, which absorb wax from the outside of the paper, will have to be replaced every few leaves or so.)

step 1

Create a base of goldenrod. Attach wire for hanging to the grapevine base (see page 11). Make bundles of goldenrod. Use glue and wire (see "Continuous Wiring" on page 13) to secure downward-hanging bundles to your wreath, hiding the stem of each bundle with the head of the next. Start at the bottom of your wreath and work your way up first one side and then the other, until you have a solid base of goldenrod.

step 2

Insert bundles and add thistles and milk pods. Make small bundles of various grasses and flowers. Arrange the bundles evenly around your wreath, gluing the stems and tucking them in between goldenrod bundles. Cut short stems of thistles and milk pods and glue them randomly around your wreath as desired.

step 3

Add wild roses, berries and bittersweet. Cut into short stems and sprigs. Insert randomly around your wreath as desired and glue into place.

step 4

Add your most delicate drieds last. Glue Queen Anne's lace, sunflowers and preserved leaves around your wreath as desired. At this point, take your wreath outside and apply a generous coat of acrylic spray to minimize shedding and help preserve the colors.

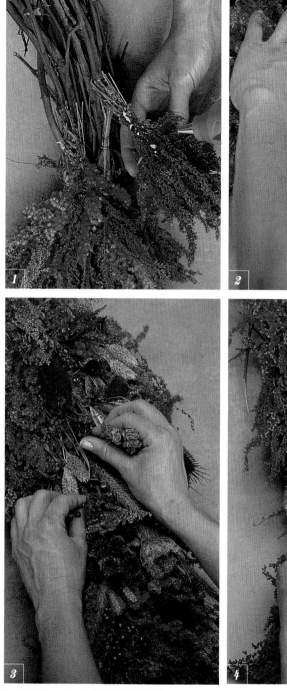

step 5

Make the bow. This bow couldn't be easier to make. Start by separating your raffia into two equal bunches. Take one length of raffia and make a loop on one end, leaving the other end hanging down as a tail. Do the same with your second length of raffia. With loops opposite each other, bring the two bunches together to form one complete bow.

step 6

And tie! Now take an extra piece of raffia and tie the two together in the center. Viola! A big raffia bow! Attach the raffia bow to the top center of your wreath using florist wire.

♦♦♦ The Country Roads Wreath—proof that one person's weed is the wreathmaker's treasure!
This wreath may shed quite a bit because of all the natural ingredients, so it's best displayed on a screened-in porch or other sheltered spot. The colors will fade and mellow with age. Personally, I like the resulting look, but if you prefer, you could always add some fresh assorted bundles and newly preserved leaves to perk it up. Or better yet, take a stroll through the country to gather the makings for your next wreath!

variation

Mountain memories
There is something about making an original piece of art out of natural "found" materials. It's like bringing a little piece of the outdoors into your home! In this case, I covered a straw base with overlapping layers of paper beech bark that had been soaked in water until pliable. Once that dried, I added fungi, moss, twigs, feathers and a neat little stone "vase" filled with a few simple dried flowers.

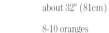

Cornhusk & Curls Wreath

what you'll need

♦♦♦ LOOK OUT ANY WINDOW OF OUR HOME AND YOU'LL SEE CORNFIELDS. I'M NEVER MORE

APPRECIATIVE OF THE VIEW THAN I AM IN THE FALL WHEN THE STALKS DRY AND MELLOW,

FORMING THE PERFECT BACKDROP FOR THE SEASON'S VIBRANT PALETTE OF ORANGES

AND GOLDS. THESE FIELDS ALSO PROVIDE ME WITH A VERY CONVENIENT SUPPLY

TIME

DIFFICULTY

OF CORNHUSK—A FAVORITE CRAFTING MATERIAL OF MINE FOR TWENTY-

FIVE YEARS. I HOPE YOU'LL TRY THIS WREATH AND DISCOVER FOR YOURSELF

THE EARTHY PLEASURE OF WORKING WITH CORNHUSK.

- twig swirl wreath, about 32" (81cm)
- 8-10 oranges
- 5 acorns and 10 acorn caps
- ten 10" (25cm) cinnamon sticks
- one bag of dried cornhusk, dyed with fabric dye (see sidebar); for a more natural wreath, leave the cornhusk un-dyed (Most craft stores sell inexpensive bags of cornhusk, but if you have permission to harvest husk from a field, remember that the fine, inner husk closest to the cob is easiest to work with.)
- brown lemon (salal) leaves
- tallow berries
- dried oak leaves
- 2 yards (1.8m) of 3" (8cm) wide burlap ribbon
- 5 small buttons
- aroma oil, clove or other autumnal scent (optional)
- ⅜" (10mm) dowel rod
- knife or peeler
- twine
- craft glue
- brown florist tape
- semi-gloss acrylic spray
- spray bottle of water
- very narrow curling iron
- florist wire
- hot glue gun

Dyeing Cornhusk

Follow the directions on the box of fabric dye, mixing colors and muting with tea bags to achieve the desired color. (Color will lighten as the husk dries.) To avoid mold, spread husks out on newspaper to dry.

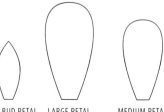

ACORN BUD PETAL   LARGE PETAL   MEDIUM PETAL   SMALL PETAL   DISK

Template for Cornhusk Flowers
Enlarge 200% to bring up to actual size.

You will need to make five flowers for this wreath. Using the templates on page 97, cut twelve large petals, ten medium petals, ten small petals and two circles per flower. Cut along the grain of the cornhusk and don't worry about cutting perfect petals—variations add to the charm of your flowers. Start by gluing together the two disks with the grains running in opposite directions for strength. (Keep the glue along the edges of the circles, because you'll be running a wire through the center later.)

> *tip*
>
> To make your cornhusk easier to work with, place it between paper towels and flatten with a dry, warm iron.

♦MAKING CORNHUSK FLOWERS

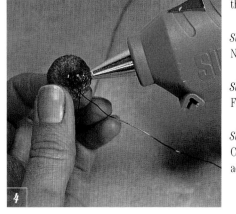

step 1
Place the base petals in two layers: glue six evenly spaced along the edge of the disk, then six more on top and between these.

step 2
Now do the same with your medium petals—two layers of five petals each.

step 3
Finally, your small petals—again, two layers of five.

step 4
Cut an 18" (46cm) length of wire. Twist the center of the wire around the "nub" of an acorn cap. Use glue to secure and allow to dry.

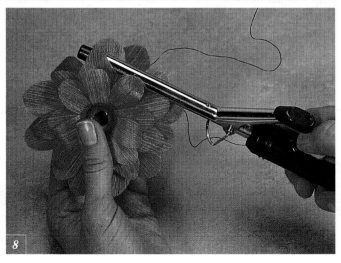

step 5
Poke both ends of the wire down through the
center of your cornhusk flower.

step 6
Use a button on the back of your flower to secure
the wire. Just run through the holes and twist,
twist, twist.

step 7
If you'd like to add a little curl to your flower, spritz
it lightly with water and allow to dry naturally.

step 8
You can also use a warm curling iron to shape
dry petals, curling the edges under slightly.

◆MAKING ACORN BUDS

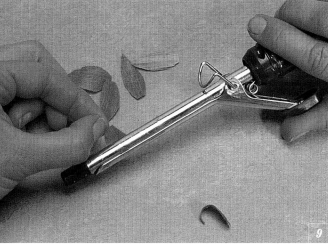

step 9
Spray five acorns with acrylic spray and allow to dry. Using the bud template on page 97, cut five to seven petals per bud. Use a warm curling iron to "flip" each petal. (Tip: If you don't have a curling iron, use twine to curl your petals around a dowel rod, spritz with water and allow to dry.)

step 10
Glue petals onto the base of your acorn.

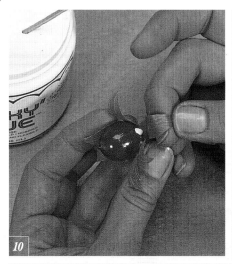

step 11
Choose caps slightly larger than your acorn buds and wire as described in step 4. Glue acorn buds into the caps.

step 12
Finish your buds by wrapping stems in brown florist tape.

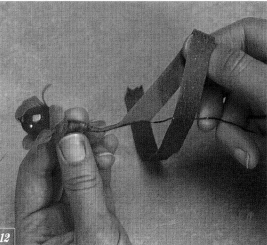

◆ MAKING ORANGE CURLS

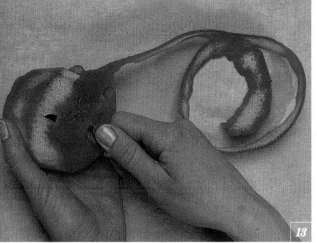

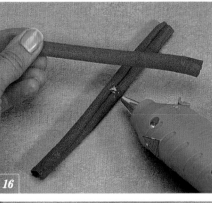

step 13

With a knife or peeler, slice long, narrow strips of peel from your orange. You can experiment with different widths to achieve different looks. You'll want about fifteen to twenty-five curls in all.

step 14

Twist the peels around the dowel, secure with a piece of twine, and allow to dry. I find that I get the best results with air-drying—especially when I set the dowels on a warm radiator. It usually takes a few days, but time will vary depending on temperature and humidity. Alternatively, you can dry the curls overnight in a very low (130°F or 55°C) oven.

step 15

Gently slip the dried curls off the dowel and apply a light coat of acrylic spray.

tip
◆

Wiping your dowel rods with just the tiniest dab of vegetable oil will make your dried curls much easier to remove.

step 16

Make cinnamon cross. Use a dab of glue to make an "X" out of two cinnamon sticks.

step 17

Make burlap bow. Make a basic bow out of a 15" (38cm) length of burlap ribbon by bringing both ends in to overlap in the middle.

step 18

Make cornhusk flower "bouquets". Layer the cornhusk flower, cinnamon stick cross and burlap bow, then use the wire from the cornhusk flower to secure. Add a dab of glue for good measure. Make five bouquets in all.

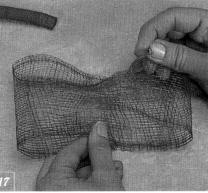

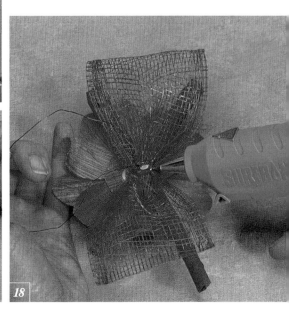

step 19
Swirl in salal. Add a dab of glue to each leaf and slip them between the twigs. Overlap leaves in a radiating pattern around the inside of your wreath. Create a second circle of salal leaves around the first one. (I used the more golden leaves from my bunch on the inner circle and the browner ones on the outside.)

step 20
Attach bouquets to wreath. Space the bouquets evenly around the inside of your wreath, using the wire stems on each bouquet to secure them in place. Attach wire for hanging (see page 11).

step 21
Add tallow berries. Glue a line of berry clusters between each cornhusk bouquet.

step 22
Add orange curls. Glue the curls radiating out from behind each bouquet.

step 23
Add acorn buds. Squeeze a dab of glue on the end of your acorn bud wires and insert them around the wreath as desired.

step 24
Finish with oak leaves and aroma. Slip the orange oak leaves between the twigs to "frame" your cornhusk flower arrangements. Use a little dab of glue to secure each one in place. If you like, apply a drop or two of aroma oil to your leaves.

♦♦♦ Enjoy your finished Cornhusk Wreath!

If you enjoyed making these simple flowers, try coming up with your own flower variations. Cornhusk is so inexpensive that you can afford to experiment. If cornhusk is not for you but you like the design of this wreath, try using dried sunflowers instead.

variation

Cornhusk & curls heart

Lemon curls and cornhusk daisies (with dried black-eyed Susan centers) add the finishing touch to this layered heart wreath. Start by placing a row of salal leaves around the inside, baby's breath on the outside, then fill in between with rows of sweet Annie, lavender and larkspur. Fill in as needed with hydrangea.

Cornucopia Dessert Wreath

♦♦♦ THIS WREATH DOES DOUBLE DUTY! USE IT AS A COLORFUL CENTERPIECE FOR THANKSGIVING DINNER, PERHAPS SURROUNDING AN ARRANGEMENT OF FRESH FLOWERS. AFTERWARD, THE WREATH BECOMES A GRAND AND EDIBLE CENTERPIECE FOR YOUR DESSERT SPREAD. IF YOU WANT TO GO ALL-OUT, CLEAN OUT A PUMPKIN TO PLACE IN THE CENTER OF YOUR WREATH AND FILL IT WITH PUNCH OR FRUIT DIP. YOU CAN ASSEMBLE THE MAJORITY OF THIS WREATH THE DAY BEFORE, PLACING THE PERISHABLE FRUITS AND FRESH FLOWERS AT THE LAST MINUTE.

TIME

DIFFICULTY

what you'll need

18" (46cm) florist wreath form with wet foam

fresh flowers and ivy leaves (I used roses and chrysanthemums)

assorted nuts (walnuts, Brazil nuts, pecans, almonds, filberts)

assortment of dessert fruits (aim for a variety of sizes and colors—I used assorted pears and apples, tangerines, grapes, plums, kumquats, strawberries and blueberries)

fresh cranberries

round toothpicks (the longer the better)

sugar glue (see recipe below)

plastic wrap

florist pins

needle and thread

Recipe for Sugar Glue

Beat one egg white until frothy. (If you prefer, use a powered egg substitute.) Add 1 cup (127g) powdered sugar, about a third at a time, beating after each addition. Beat five minutes longer until stiff.

tips

• To give your fruit a bit of sheen, polish with a paper towel and just a dab of vegetable oil.

• To protect your table from any moisture, place a pad or folded towel under the tablecloth.

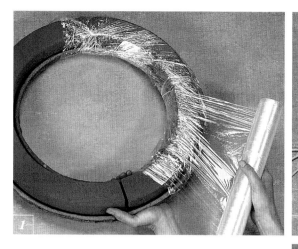

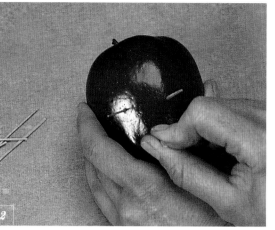

step 1
Prepare oasis. Immerse florist foam in water until saturated and wrap with plastic wrap.

step 2
"Pick" your largest fruit first. A good, general rule for assembling this wreath is to work from your largest ingredient to your smallest. So starting with your biggest fruit—in my case the red apples—insert two or three toothpicks, which you'll use to anchor your fruit in the foam.

step 3
Nestle in apples. Place four apples evenly spaced around the top of your wreath. Don't be afraid to push—the idea is to "nestle" your fruit into the foam, using the toothpicks to hold the fruit in place. Think of your wreath in fourths, adding about the same amount of each fruit to each quadrant to achieve a full, balanced look.

step 4
"Pick" and place apples and pears.
Fill in the top of your wreath with larger fruit, leaving space to add flowers later.

tip

Don't place your fruits to sit perfectly straight; you'll get a more pleasing effect by angling them this way and that.

step 5

Add a ring of ivy leaves. Using florist pins, cover the lower
edge with a skirt of slightly overlapping ivy leaves. This will
camouflage the wreath form and create a nice, finished look.

step 6

"Pick" and place fruit. Using picks, place the brown
pears, green apples, tangerines and plums randomly around
your wreath. Fill in the side of your wreath, leaving space to
add flowers.

step 7

Add flowers. Now it's time to fill in those spaces you've been
saving. Holding the stems under water, cut them down to
about 4" (10cm). Use needlenose pliers to poke holes in your
foam and insert flowers.

step 8

Go nuts! Arrange the nuts around your wreath. Some will nestle between fruits. Otherwise, use a dab of sugar glue to hold in place.

step 9

Weave in cranberry garland. Using a needle and thread, string four 2' (1.2m) lengths of cranberries. Weave the cranberry garland between and around your fruits, securing the ends with florist pins.

step 10

Accent with smallest fruits. Pick and place kumquats. Break grapes into small clusters and arrange around the top of the wreath. Skewer two or three blueberries per toothpick and insert around wreath as desired.

step 11

Finish with ivy leaves. Just slip a few ivy leaves around your flowers, and you're set!

♦♦♦ A grand finale!

Now if only everyone can save room for dessert! Not just for Thanksgiving, this wreath will make any occasion—from casual summer barbecue to formal affair—feel special. For a variation, you can apply the same idea on a smaller scale using vegetables to dress up individual place settings. Form a circle out of a piece of heavy wire, sized to fit around a small bowl or custard cup. Using fine green wire, cover the circle with fresh parsley, then decorate with mini carrots, radish "roses", olives, cherry tomatoes, etc. Add dip and serve!

Merry Winter

♦♦♦ The smell of fresh pine, snow falling soft as a lullaby, baking cookies into the wee hours of the morning…Factor in winter's sleigh-full of wreath-makings—from ivy and poinsettia to jingle bells and gingerbread men—and it truly is the most wonderful time of the year!

In this season of decorating merriment, anything goes for wreaths. Deck them out in traditional greens and reds, magical silvers and golds, Victorian mauves and pinks, or a sweet, candy-colored palette.

If you're short on time (and who isn't this time of year?) you'll appreciate the Winter Berry and Sugarplums wreaths. Short on gifts for the names on your list? You can make a Glitter 'n' Glow Candle Ring in the time it takes you to find a parking spot at the mall! For full-fledged winter romance, there's the Let-It-Snow Chandelier and the Sweetheart Wreath, both at the very top of the mood-setting scale.

(above) LET-IT-SNOW CHANDELIER; (opposite page starting from upper left, clockwise) GLITTER 'N GLOW CANDLE RING, SUGARPLUMS WREATH, SWEETHEART WREATH, WINTER BERRY WREATH

Winter Berry Wreath

what you'll need

♦♦♦ HERE'S A CHRISTMAS QUICKIE! DECORATE A PLAIN BAY LEAF BASE WITH GARLANDS OF

IVORY LACE AND PEPPERBERRIES…SUSPEND IT FROM A DECKED-OUT BOW…AND

TIME

BEFORE YOU KNOW IT, YOU'LL BE LOOKING AT A WREATH-FULL OF CHRISTMAS

DIFFICULTY

CHEER. JUST ADD MULLED APPLE CIDER, A CRACKLING FIRE AND HOLIDAY

SINGING IN THE BACKGROUND, AND YOU'VE GOT ALL THE MAKINGS OF AN

EVENING OF OLD-FASHIONED HOLIDAY ROMANCE.

16" (41cm) bay leaf wreath

dried cedar

ivory lace (you can substitute
baby's breath or candy tuft)

pepperberries (red)

mini pinecones

burgundy brunia flowers
(you can substitute canella
berries or mini rosebuds)

5 freeze-dried rose heads (ivory)

4 yards (3.6m) of 1½" (3.8cm)
wired ivory satin ribbon

2 yards (1.8m) of narrow ribbon

florist wire

hot glue gun

step 1

Work in cedar. Start by adding a little extra texture to your bay leaf wreath by gluing sprigs of cedar throughout.

step 2

Plan your pattern. Swirl a narrow piece of ribbon around your wreath to indicate where you will place your flowers. Leave space at the top to add your roses later.

step 3

Start with the ivory lace. Using the ribbon as a guide, glue in your ivory lace sprig by sprig. (Do not bundle—you're aiming for a more elongated effect.) Remove the ribbon as you go.

step 4

Glue in clusters of pepperberries. Aim to create the impression of a pepperberry garland twisting around the ivory lace.

step 5

Add pinecones. Glue the mini pinecones in clusters of two or three, concentrating them along the edges of your "garlands."

step 6

Make "holly berry" clusters. Wire a cluster of three brunia flowers together by the stems, then add a dab of glue to secure. (Okay, they're not really holly berries. But who's to know?)

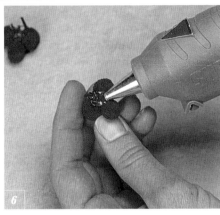

step 7

Glue on berry clusters. Concentrate the clusters around the pinecones.

step 8

Add roses. Arrange the roses at the top of your wreath and glue into place.

step 9

Accent with pinecones and berry clusters. Really make your roses "pop" by filling in around them with pinecones and berry clusters.

step 10

Make hanging ribbon. Make a stacked bow (see page 14) leaving 15" (38cm) long tails. Make a 1½" (4cm) hanging hoop out of heavy wire. (Wrap the wire around two fingers three times, then twist with an additional wire to secure.) Attach the hoop to the back of your bow with a piece of narrow ribbon.

step 11

Attach ribbon. Carefully flip your wreath over. With the bow centered directly above your roses and a few inches above the top edge of your wreath, glue the tails trailing down each side. Reinforce in two or three spots per side with wire—double the wire, thread under the wreath frame and twist securely.

step 12

Fancify bow. Add a little arrangement of pinecones, brunia clusters and bay leaves to the center of your bow.

♦♦♦ A whirl of Christmas cheer!
There you have it—and with plenty
of time left to finish wrapping your
gifts! Now that you know how easy
it is to dress up a plain wreath, you
can add a swirl of color to any season!
Come spring, I think I'll try pink
baby's breath and globe amaranth
in assorted pastels. Yellow caspia,
bittersweet and tallow berries would
make a pretty variation for fall.

variation

Same swirl, different stuff
You really need to start with a nice base to pull
off this type of wreath, since sections are left
exposed. An airy fern wreath was the inspiration
for this whirl of pink, featuring pink rodanthe,
burgundy sweet Annie, pink rice flowers and
yellow strawflowers.

Glitter 'n' Glow Candle Ring

♦♦♦ THIS FESTIVE LITTLE WREATH TURNS AN ORDINARY GLASS HURRICANE INTO A SPARKLING

CENTERPIECE—THE PERFECT TOUCH OF CHRISTMAS CHEER FOR YOUR COFFEE TABLE.

DURING THE DAY, THE RICH PINKS AND GOLDS BRIGHTEN ANY ROOM. AT NIGHT, WHEN

TIME

THE CANDLELIGHT STRIKES, YOU'LL LOVE THE DAZZLE OF THE GLITTER AND THE

DIFFICULTY

GLOW OF THE GLASS BULBS. AND COME GIFT-GIVING TIME, THIS GEM OF A

WREATH IS PERFECT FOR THE FRIENDS ON YOUR LIST—IT'S SO QUICK TO MAKE

AND A CINCH TO CUSTOMIZE USING THEIR FAVORITE COLORS!

grapevine wreath—I used
a 9" (23cm) wreath, but choose
the size that best accommodates
your hurricane

dried sweet Annie (burgundy)

dried hydrangea (light green/pink)

six 1" (2.5cm) glass ball ornaments

12 small pinecones

12 acorns

coxcomb

pepperberries (pink)

preserved cedar (gold)

grapevine tendrils

gold spray paint (I prefer the
14K gold kind for more sheen)

pink spray paint

very fine glitter

hurricane

florist wire

acrylic spray

hot glue gun

tip
♦

Dried materials are highly
flammable. Always use a hurricane
with this wreath—never use it
directly surrounding a lit candle.

step 1

Spray wreath. Spray your wreath with gold paint. While you're at it, spray your cedar, pinecones, acorns and grapevine tendrils. Allow to dry.

step 2

Start with cedar and sweet Annie. Fill in the bottom of your wreath in a radiating pattern, alternating sprigs of cedar and sweet Annie.

step 3

Add hydrangea. Tint hydrangea with a light dusting of pink spray paint. Break the hydrangea into small pieces and use it to fill in the top of your wreath. (See page 13 for special tips on working with hydrangea.) Remember—your hurricane will be in the center, so there's no need to cover the inner perimeter.

step 4

Add glass balls. Arrange glass balls around your wreath as desired. Once you're happy with the spacing, glue into place.

step 5

Wiring pinecones. Use a wire that is strong enough to hold the pinecone, but fine enough to slip between the petals. Simply work the wire in between petals at the base of the pinecone and twist to secure. Trim wire, leaving enough to attach the pinecone to your wreath.

step 6

Add pinecones. Use wire stems to secure the pinecones here and there around the wreath.

step 7

Add acorns. Cluster acorns, cap down, around your wreath.

step 8

Add coxcomb. Break into small pieces and glue around wreath as desired.

step 9

Add pepperberries. Break pepperberries into small clusters and glue around the wreath as desired. Be sure to fill in any sparse spots.

step 10
Glitter up! Spray your wreath with a light coat of acrylic spray and immediately sprinkle with glitter.

step 11
Top with tendrils. Glue gold tendrils randomly around the wreath. Don't nestle them too far down—let them stick out to add texture and dimension to your wreath. The only thing missing now is a candle in your favorite Christmas aroma!

♦♦♦ Glimmer, shimmer and glow!
I love the pink and gold tones of
this candle ring—but when you
make yours, use whatever colors
tickle your fancy, from silver mono-
tones to a mix of glorious jewel
tones. You can follow the same
directions to create a full-sized wall
wreath—just be sure to fill in the
inner perimeter with hydrangea.

variation

Glittery wall wreath
I love this festive combination of dried red roses,
rice flowers, pepperberries, pinecones (painted
with artificial snow) and seashells. Pearly balls
and snowflakes (they're actually buttons!) are
icing on the cake. Start by covering a little straw
base with preserved cedar, and finish with a generous sprinkling of glitter.

Sugarplums Wreath

what you'll need

♦♦♦ IF YOU'RE SHORT ON TIME BUT BIG ON CHRISTMAS, HERE'S A SPECIAL GIFT FROM ME TO YOU: A QUICK AND WHIMSICAL WAY TO DRESS UP A PLAIN EVERGREEN WREATH! PART OF THE BEAUTY OF THIS DESIGN IS THAT, AFTER CHRISTMAS, YOU CAN SIMPLY REPLACE THE CENTER HOOP WITH A MORE GENERIC WINTER-THEMED ONE. THAT WAY, YOU GET MORE USE OUT OF YOUR PRETTY EVERGREEN WREATH, AND YOUR FAMILY DOESN'T MOCK YOU FOR LEAVING CHRISTMAS DECORATIONS UP THROUGH FEBRUARY!

TIME

DIFFICULTY

24" (61cm) fresh or artificial evergreen wreath (use a wreath pre-strung with lights for additional twinkle)

metal hoop—I used a 12" (31cm) hoop, but you should choose a ring slightly larger than the center of your wreath

3 yards (2.7m) of inexpensive, 1" (2.5cm) green ribbon

7 yards (6.3m) wired 1½" (3.8cm) red satin ribbon

3½ yards (3.2m) wired 1½" (4cm) sheer red ribbon

artificial candy picks—I used 25, but how many you need will vary depending on the size of your picks and hoop

8 beaded berry picks

16 candy canes

8 rubber bands

8 peppermint sticks

1 stem of white glitter stars

florist wire

hot glue gun

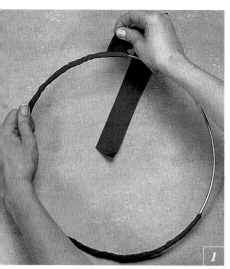

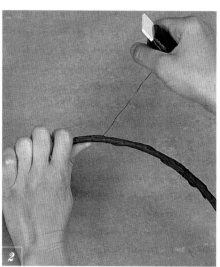

step 1

Wrap hoop in ribbon. Instead of trying to wrap the entire hoop with one continuous piece of ribbon, cut your ribbon into 2' to 3' (61cm to 91cm) lengths, securing the ends with glue. Don't worry about being perfect here. You're just trying to camouflage the hoop. As long as no gold shows, you're set.

step 2

Use wire to secure ribbon. Wrap, wrap, wrap, spiraling the wire around your hoop every inch (2.5cm) or two to hold the ribbon in place.

step 3

Tie on ribbons. Cut 15" (38cm) pieces of ribbon—sixteen satin and eight sheer. Sandwich one sheer piece between two satin pieces and tie onto your hoop, leaving about twice as much on the outside as on the inside. (No need to measure—just eye it.) Tie on the remaining ribbons the same way, evenly spacing them around the hoop.

step 4

Now for the candy! If necessary, trim the stems of your picks down to 2" or 3" (5cm or 8cm) to make them easier to work with. Using continuous wiring (see page 13), attach your candy picks to the front of your hoop. (Careful not to catch your ribbons in the wire!)

step 5

Add mounting wires. Cut four 3' (91cm) pieces of heavy wire and attach them evenly around the back of your hoop. Thread each wire under the hoop and twist so that you're left with two equal tails.

step 6

Mount hoop on wreath. Center the hoop on the front of your evergreen and attach with the wires. (Don't cut the excess wire, just tuck it in so you can remove the hoop and re-use it next year.)

step 7

Add berries. Slip in berry picks, centered at each ribbon. Use the stem of the pick or a piece of wire to secure.

step 8

Make candy cane hearts. Use a rubber band to connect two candy canes at the base. Angle the tops of the candy canes to form a heart shape and add a dab of glue to secure. Hold for a minute or two until the glue sets. Repeat with the rest of your candy canes to make eight hearts in all.

step 9

Attach hearts. Twist a piece of wire around the rubber bands at the base of your hearts. Position hearts between ribbons and secure with wire.

step 10

Now the peppermint sticks. Work in the peppermint sticks evenly around your wreath, slipping between candies to hold in place.

step 11

Finish with glittery stars. Clip off individual stars, leaving a wire stem on each. Glue the stars randomly around your wreath. Let them extend above the candy picks rather than nestling them in the wreath.

◆◆◆ **Sweet!**

Shape the ribbons into nice, neat waves and hang the wreath. If only gift-shopping were this quick and easy! After the holidays, all it takes is a few minutes to remove the sugarplum hoop, pack it away for next year, and replace it with a hoop of your choice—say a simple hoop of pinecones or a romantic ring of poinsettias.

variation

Even simpler!

A hoop, some glittery silk rose picks and an evergreen base. Put them all together, and you've got a simply elegant display for Thanksgiving through Valentine's Day!

Let-It-Snow Chandelier

what you'll need

♦♦♦ WHEN THE WEATHER OUTSIDE IS FRIGHTFUL, THIS CHANDELIER IS SO DELIGHTFUL. IT'S GUARANTEED TO ADD A WARM GLOW TO EVEN THE CHILLIEST EVENING. TURN ON THE

TIME

DIFFICULTY

TWINKLE LIGHTS AND YOU'RE CAST INTO A WINTER WONDERLAND, COMPLETE WITH GLIMMERING SNOWFLAKES AND THE LIVELY SHADOWS OF BRANCHES DANCING ACROSS THE WALLS. IT'S SO FANTASTIC, SO FANCIFUL, YOU'LL HATE TO PUT IT AWAY COME SPRING!

24" (61cm) artificial
evergreen wreath

glittered grapes,
or use ½" (1.3cm)
glittered glass balls

2 silver berry garlands

2 bunches of dried baby's breath—
one silver, one glittered

15 glass berries

5-10 very fine branches

15 medium silver glass
ball ornaments

glitter snow

very fine silver glitter

three 10-light strings of
battery-operated twinkle lights
(NOTE: Use more or less, depending
on the effect you're after. Personally,
I like not having a cord to worry
about. But if you prefer, use a regular string of twinkle lights or a
pre-strung wreath, running the
cord up one of the braided ribbons.)

12 yards (10.8m) of sheer
white wired ribbon

7 yards (6.3m) of tulle for bows

12 snowflake ornaments

white spray paint

1" (3cm) welded O-ring

fishing line and ornament hooks

florist wire

hot glue gun

◆ MAKING SNOWBALLS

step 1
Secure the cap to the ornament with a dab of hot glue.

step 2
Squeeze a dab of glue onto the wire as well to ensure your finished "snowball" stays securely in place. (You want to create the impression of falling snow, not falling ornaments!) Twist a piece of wire (about 18" [46cm]) onto the cap; you'll use this to attach the finished snowball to your wreath.

step 3
Paint the top half of your ball with glitter snow to create the impression of snow. Your snowball will be embedded in the wreath, so paint down at least halfway for the best effect. Move on to the next step before your snow dries!

step 4
While the snow is still wet, glitz it up with a little extra glitter.

step 5
Snip your grapes and one of your berry garlands into individual pieces. (Save the second garland to use in step 15.) Glue about five or six grapes randomly around your bulb, about one-third of the way down from the top.

step 6
Fill in between with the berries. Allow to dry overnight.

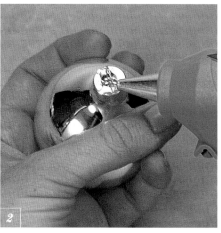

tip
◆

Make your first "snowball" bundle start to finish for practice. Then divide your materials for the remaining bundles and do assembly line construction. You'll be surprised how fast it goes!

step 7

Secure the lights. Arrange the battery boxes for your lights on the back of your wreath. (This will be the top of your chandelier.) I've grouped mine together to make them more convenient to switch on and off. Secure the boxes in place by wiring to the wire wreath base.

step 8

Weave in the lights. Distribute lights evenly around your wreath. Pull the lights down so they show on the front of your wreath (the bottom of your chandelier), which is the angle from which your chandelier will primarily be viewed. Wire cords every few inches to hold in place.

step 9

Make braids for hanging. Cut three 2½" (6cm) lengths of ribbon. Securely fasten the ends of the ribbons with a 10" (25cm) piece of wire. (Don't trim off the excess wire yet, you'll be using it in the next step!) Braid the ribbons together tightly and secure the end with a second piece of wire. Repeat three times to create four braids in total.

step 10

Attach one end to wreath. Spacing your braids evenly around the wreath, loop one end around the wire wreath base and secure with excess wire. Add a dab of glue for good measure.

---

tip

Step Saver

Use chain in place of the ribbon braids for hanging your chandelier.

step 11

Attach other end to O-ring. Use excess wire to attach the top ends of your braids to the O-ring. Take a minute to ensure that they are of equal length and not crossing over each other so that your chandelier will hang level.

step 12

Top with ribbon curls. To soften and disguise the point where you tied your braids to the O-ring: Cut remaining ribbon into 10" (25cm) pieces and curl around your finger to shape. With a piece of wire at the center, attach the ribbons at the very top of your braids and arrange.

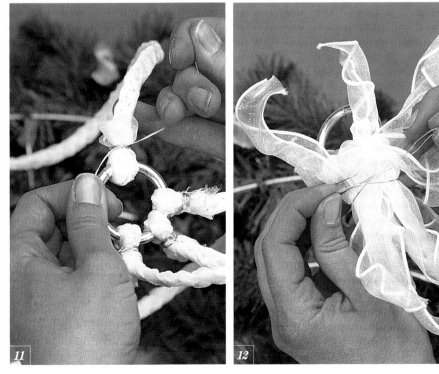

step 13

Attach "snowballs". Stagger snowballs around the front of your wreath. Once you're happy with placement, use wires to secure to the wreath but not too tight—you want them to hang down far enough from your chandelier so those sparkly clusters are visible.

step 14

Add a blizzard of baby's breath. Make small bundles of silver and glittery baby's breath, and use to fill in around your snowballs and throughout your wreath.

step 15

Accent with silver and glass berries. Snip your remaining berry garland into 3" or 4" (8cm or 10cm) sprigs and glue around your wreath, concentrating them on the outer perimeter. Do the same with your glass berries, adding in small clusters. At this point, suspend your chandelier to proceed.

step 16

Top with snow-covered branches. Spray your branches white and allow to dry. (If you like, you can add to the snowy effect by touching up your branches with glitter snow!) Slip the branches in around the top of your chandelier, angling them slightly inward. (Skip the glue for easier storage of your wreath.)

step 17

Finish with drifts of tulle. Cut your tulle into fourths. Tie a simple bow onto the base of each braid, leaving 25" (64cm) tails. Arrange the tails to lie between the wreath and the branches. This softens the transition and helps to hide the light boxes.

step 18

Now, just add snow! Suspend your snowflakes at varying heights around your wreath using fishing line. (Tie one end to an ornament hook.)

tip

Add extra glimmer to your snowflakes with Plaid's Gallery Glass Crystal Beads. Look for them in the glass painting section of your local craft store.

♦♦♦ **Bask in the glow of your finished Winter Chandelier!** This chandelier makes charming mood lighting above a table or a cozy welcome in a foyer or bay window. At the end of the season, simply slip out the branches, unhook the snowflakes, and store the wreath upside-down to avoid crushing the flowers and glass balls.

variation

Falling leaves

Pick your favorite silk or velvet leaves for this colorful fall chandelier wreath! The base is an inexpensive grapevine wreath. For the falling leaves, I glued my single-sided velvet leaves back to back. Instead of twinkle lights, I glued canning jar rings around the top of my wreath to anchor votive candles. The best part—no raking!

Sweetheart Wreath

what you'll need

♦♦♦ THIS WREATH IS ONLY FOR THE UTTERLY ROMANTIC AT HEART. SUGARY PINK FREEZE-DRIED ROSES AND A SWEET LITTLE BOX OF CANDIES ARE DELIVERED WITH LOVE ON A SATIN-WRAPPED HEART. WITH THE ROSES SIMPLY PINNED IN PLACE, THIS WREATH MAKES AN EXTRA-SPECIAL GIFT—ESPECIALLY FOR FELLOW CRAFTERS WHO CAN REMOVE THE ROSES AFTER VALENTINE'S DAY FOR USE IN THEIR NEXT PROJECT…PERHAPS A GIFT FOR YOU! EVEN THE LEAST CRAFTY RECIPIENT CAN USE THE ROSES IN POTPOURRI OR SIMPLY ARRANGE THEM IN A PRETTY BOWL.

TIME

DIFFICULTY

- 18" (46cm) foam heart
- 6" x 1" (15cm x 2.5cm) round florist foam
- 12 freeze-dried roses—pink, 1½" to 2" heads (3.8cm to 5cm), or use silk or velvet rose heads
- assorted dried fillers (baker's fern, baby's breath, caspia)
- 12 rose stems
- 9 yards (8.1m) of 1½" (3.8cm) satin ribbon (wine) for wrapping base
- 3½ yards (3.2m) of ⅞" (2.2cm) organza ribbon (wine) for bow
- aroma oil—rose or other "romantic" fragrance (optional)
- 2 sheets of patterned tissue paper
- small heart-shaped paper doilies
- shallow, heart-shaped box with lid, about 5" (13cm) wide (papier mâché or any lightweight material)
- artificial candies—I made truffles out of polymer clay, topped with candy sprinkles—or wrap small foam balls in candy foils (If you're making this as a gift wreath, you may want to attach a real box of chocolates!)
- polyester fill
- pink spray paint
- white acrylic paint
- decorative-edge scissors
- embossing foil and stylus
- florist pins
- hot glue gun
- rubber bands
- small sponge

Template for embossed gift tag

step 1

Begin wrapping points in ribbon. Cut two pieces of satin ribbon, about 6" (15cm) each. Arrange ribbons along either side of the top point as shown, gluing ends on the opposite side of the wreath. Do the same for the bottom point, then flip the wreath over (this will be the front of your finished wreath) and repeat, being sure to glue ribbon on the opposite side. It may look messy now, but trust me—it will pay off.

step 2

Finish points. Now cover each point with three short, slightly overlapped horizontal ribbons as shown. Again, secure all ends on the opposite side of the wreath, and finish both points on the back of your wreath before doing the front points.

step 3

Wrap it up. Now that the points are taken care of, the rest of the wreath should be a piece of cake! Wrap each side of your heart with a continuous length of satin ribbon, keeping a taught and even overlap. Secure each end on the back of the wreath with a dab of glue. Add two wires at the top of your heart for hanging. (See page 11 for instructions.)

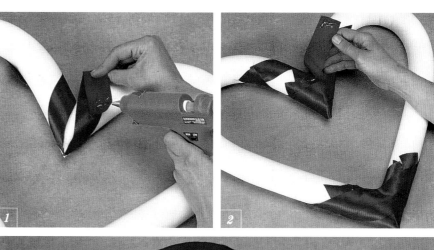

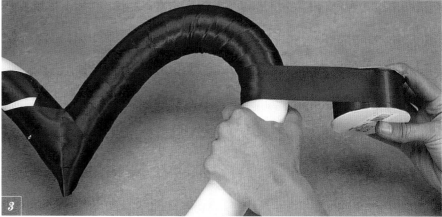

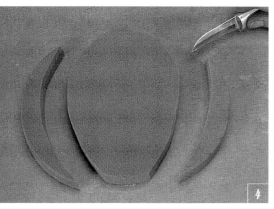

(See page 11 for instructions.)

tip

If your ribbon attracts lint try spraying it with a static removal spray.

step 4

Shape base for bouquet. Cut your florist foam into an oval shape.

step 5

Attach roses. Arrange your roses on the oval base, using florist pins to secure. (Skipping the glue means the roses can be removed and reused.)

step 6

Add caspia and baby's breath. Fill in around the roses with sprigs of caspia and baby's breath. To maintain the "removability" of the roses, take care to glue these fillers to the foam and not to the roses.

step 7

Attach stems. Use a rubber band to bundle together the rose stems. Insert into the bottom edge of the florist foam.

step 8

Arrange tissue. Place both pieces of tissue paper (wrong sides together) under your arrangement. Lie your bouquet diagonally on your tissue. Add a strip of polyester fill along the stems to give them more bulk.

step 9

Fold over tissue. Fold up the bottom point of the tissue to form a triangle behind your bouquet, leaving 1"–2" (3cm–5cm) of stems exposed at bottom. Trim off excess tissue. Wrap your bouquet in the tissue like you'd wrap a baby in a blanket—fold in one side, and then the other. Roll down the top of the tissue to frame your bouquet. Glue tissue to the back of florist foam and secure with a few florist pins.

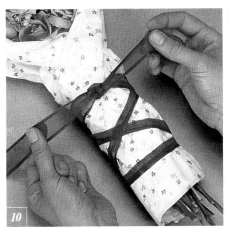

step 10

Wrap stems with ribbon. Cut a piece of organza ribbon about 24" (61cm) long. Starting with the center of the ribbon at the bottom of your stems, criss-cross up and around as shown. When you reach the top of your stems, tie the ribbon off in a square knot.

step 11

Add a bow. Make a stacked bow of organza ribbon (see page 14) and tie on using tails from the square knot. Position the bouquet diagonally across the heart and secure in place with florist pins and hot glue. (If you like, you can skip the glue so the entire bouquet can be removed and used as a pretty tabletop display.)

step 12

Add sprigs of baker's fern. Arrange around the outside of the bouquet, taking care to glue them to the tissue or the florist foam and not the roses.

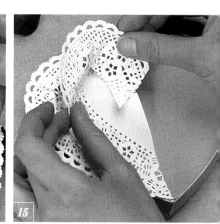

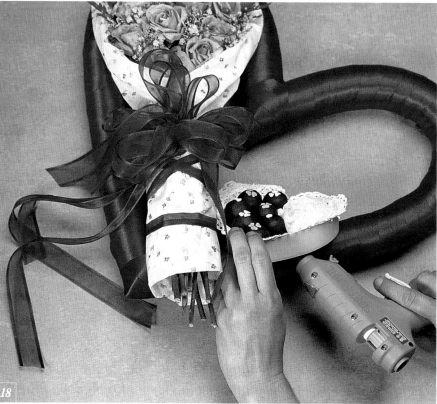

step 13
Paint heart box. Apply a light coat of spray paint to the box and lid. Repeat as necessary, allowing to dry between coats.

step 14
Stencil box design. Center your doily on your box lid. Use white acrylic paint to sponge over the doily and transfer the pattern to your box lid. (Before stenciling your lid, it's a good idea to practice on a piece of scrap cardboard first.)

step 15
Line box with doilies. Unless your doily fits your box perfectly, you'll have to do some cutting and piecing here. Just remember that the left side will show and the right side will be hidden under the lid.

step 16
Truffle time! Now arrange and glue your candies in the left side of your box. You can cheat and fill the right side with tissue—nobody will ever know.

step 17
Emboss gift tag. Cut a 2½" (6cm) square of embossing foil using your decorative-edge scissors. Use your stylus and the pattern on page 137 (or your own original design) to emboss your gift tag. It's a good idea to do this on top of a thick piece of cardboard, a section of newspaper or some other surface that has some give.

step 18
Attach box of candies. Experiment with your candy box until you find the placement and angle you like best. Glue onto wreath and hold in place for a few minutes while it dries.

step 19

Add lid, gift tag and aroma. Now glue the lid atop your box and tie on the gift tag. If you like, add a drop of two of aroma oil behind the roses.

♦♦♦ **Valentine romance, straight from the heart!**
Pinning in the roses is not only a great perk for gift-giving, as I've already mentioned. It's also a clever way to "renew" this wreath every year. Simply pin in a fresh dozen roses every Valentine's Day—the rest of the wreath should hold up just fine.

variation

Spread a little love!
You can make sweet little hearts like these in no time! Gather small foam hearts, pretty ribbons and assorted dried flowers and spend a fun afternoon making mini Valentine wreaths for all your friends. They make great decorations for gift-wrapping, too!

Resources

Flyboy Naturals

15550 Old Highway 99 South
Myrtle Creek, OR 97457
(800) 465-5125
Fax: (541) 863-7757
E-mail: flyboy@wizzards.net
www.flyboynaturals.com
♦ specializes in freeze-dried flowers, fruits
and vegetables

D&P Flowers

3657 G 7/10 Rd.
Palisade, CO 81526
(970) 464-0558
Fax: (970) 464-5332
E-mail: dpflo1000@aol.com
www.dpflowers.com
♦ specializes in naturally dried and
freeze-dried flowers

Flying B Bar Ranch

1100 McMullen Creek Rd.
Selma, OR 97538
(541) 597-2418
Fax: (541) 597-2050
E-mail: roses@webtrail.com
www.webtrail.com/roses
♦ specializes in freeze-dried garden roses;
carries over 60 different varieties

The Flower Mart.com

P.O. Box 1809
Hillsboro, OR 97123
(800) 733-0506
Fax: (503) 628-0647
E-mail: sales@theflowermart.com
www.theflowermart.com
♦ specialists in fine dried and preserved florals

Dried Flowers Direct

3597 Skyline Dr.
Penn Yann, NY 14527
(315) 536-2736
E-mail: drieds@linkny.com
www.driedflowersdirect.com
♦ growers of wholesale and retail dried flowers
from Keuka Flower Farm

Donna's Weed Barn

Route 985
Boswell, PA 15531
(814) 629-6708
♦ dried flowers and floral supplies